AN iGEN COOKBOOK

THE UNSKILLED

A Delicious Crash Course

Written by Lavinia M. Hughes

An iGen Cookbook for the Unskilled

Lavinia M. Hughes

Published by Waquoit Wordsmith Press, 2021.

AN IGEN COOKBOOK FOR THE UNSKILLED

First edition. November 18, 2021.

Copyright © 2021 Lavinia M. Hughes.

ISBN: 979-8201691301

Written by Lavinia M. Hughes.

Also by Lavinia M. Hughes

Enter Through the Crawlspace
An iGen Cookbook for the Unskilled

Table of Contents

This book is dedicated to my wonderful husband Richard, who is the happy and principal taste tester of the recipes in this book.

"My definition of man is a cooking animal. The beasts have memory, judgment, and the faculties and passions of our minds in a certain degree; but no beast is a cook."

— James Boswell, *The Journals*, 1762-95[1]

1. https://www.goodreads.com/work/quotes/156006

INFORMATION AND RECIPES

———

INTRODUCTION

═══

THIS COOKBOOK IS FOR:

- **Teenagers**
- **Young adults**
- **A person of any age who never learned to cook**
- **A person of any age looking for inspiration**
- **Those looking for easy-to-follow recipes that don't have 700 ingredients or 3 pages of directions**
- **People looking for handy hints on entertaining**

Greetings, potential chefs. Chef is a big word, but after you master the basics of cooking and move onto some of my advanced recipes (just a few, I promise), you will feel like a chef.

Why learn to cook? Can't you just let someone else do it—your significant other, parent, sibling, roommate? Sure, if you want to stoke resentment in these relationships. Do they notice that you always eat, but are never part of the party when it comes to food preparation? Oh, yeah, they do.

Why not just eat convenience foods? I love a good TV dinner now and then. But they're not exactly health foods, instead, usually heavily processed with too many calories and too much sodium.

Why not just eat out every meal? Is your last name Vanderbilt, Rockefeller, or Kardashian? If it is, you are free to eat every meal at a restaurant or rely on your personal chef to whip up something nice at your mansion. If it's not your last name and you're broke from regularly paying $9.95 for a grilled cheese sandwich, you need to learn how to cook. I am not disparaging a restaurant from charging almost $10 for a simple grilled cheese sandwich, by the way. They have operating expenses added to their food cost, so they have to charge a premium. But FYI, the cost of making a grilled cheese sandwich at home is only about 49 cents. My recipe for making the perfect grilled cheese sandwich is found later on in this book in the Miscellaneous section. In my experience, only one restaurant in my town of Falmouth, Massachusetts, makes it better than I do. It's called Country Fare and it's awesome.

Cooking allows you to be creative and put your own personal stamp on it, as they always say in those ubiquitous home renovation shows.

Make something delicious, learn new things, entertain family and friends, and eat better. Every recipe you try is a learning experience. The technique you learn in one recipe can be applied to other recipes.

I'll start with a section on cookware and tools, follow up with a section on food safety, then there will be a chapter on each category of food. Each recipe will be clearly laid out with ingredients, instructional steps, a few cooking terms, what bowls and pans you should set out, and notes and tips. Sometimes it helps to know why you have to do a certain thing.

I encourage you to organize your own cooking efforts with a recipe box or 3-ring binder. Try the recipe exactly as written. If, after trying it the first time, you prefer to do it another way or use different ingredients, make a note on the recipe.

I don't like fresh garlic and I never use it. Occasionally I will put in a dash of garlic powder. That's my preference. If you like fresh garlic, feel free to add it.

It should also be noted here that you can make many changes in a recipe for main or savory dishes and it won't necessarily affect the outcome. But sauces and baked goods usually need to be made in the exact amounts of the recipe or they won't be right. Until you have more experience, this is a good rule to follow.

COOKWARE AND TOOLS

———

HERE IS A LIST OF BASIC items you should have in your kitchen. If you're living at home, have a spouse, or a roommate, you probably have a lot of these things. Having the right tool does make food preparation easier, faster, and more fun. I just got an immersion blender for a gift and I love it. A thrift store has many of these items, often in excellent condition, for an affordable price.

It helps to have multiples of things like measuring cups and spatulas. You'll use them.

If you buy a typical full set of pots and pans, it will have:

> Large frying pan with cover

> Small frying pan with cover

> Large saucepan with cover (3 quart). Capacity is usually stamped on the bottom

> Small saucepan with cover – 1-1/2 quart

> Dutch oven – a kind of squat stockpot OR

> Stockpot – 8 quart. High sides for boiling lobsters, making large amounts of soup

Other items you'll want:

- Au gratin pan – metal pan used for putting under broiler
- Non-stick pan for omelettes
- Casserole dishes with cover - in several sizes
- Set of various-sized mixing bowls
- 13" x 9" baking dish in glass and one in metal
- Cookie sheets in several sizes (aka "sheet pans")
- Two round cake pans 8" or 9"
- Two square cake pans 8" or 9" (aka "brownie pan")
- Two pie plates
- Metal racks for roasting and wire racks for cooling
- Two sets of measuring spoons
- Two sets of measuring cups
- Glass measuring cups in various sizes
- Several cutting boards, one for vegetables, one for poultry, etc.
- Two loaf pans
- Muffin tins of various sizes (also buy paper liners to fit)
- Strainers in various sizes
- Airtight canisters for flour, sugar, pancake mix, dried peas, etc.
- Oven mitts

Utensils:

- ❖ Wire whisks

- ❖ Lemon zester

- ❖ Vegetable peeler

- ❖ Silicone brush

- ❖ Flipper for pancakes, burgers, etc.

- ❖ Tongs

- ❖ Pasta fork for serving

- ❖ Rubber spatulas

- ❖ Wooden spoons

- ❖ Slotted spoons

- ❖ Meat tenderizer mallet

- ❖ Ice cream scoops, (aka portion-control scoop

- ❖ Set of cutlery knives

- ❖ Food thermometer (different from candy thermometer) – for meat

- ❖ Grapefruit knives and grapefruit spoons

Appliances/Motorized Things:

- ❑ Food processor with various attachments for grating and slicing

- ❑ Mini-chopper

- ❑ Blender

- ❑ Mixer – either a countertop one if you have the room, or a hand mixer

- ❑ Immersion blender – my favorite tool!

FOOD SAFETY

THIS IS NOT AN EXHAUSTIVE lesson on food safety. Years ago, I completed a Serv-Safe certification course given by the Massachusetts Department of Agriculture, which was a total of about 12 hours of in-person instruction. Today, its online course is just a few hours for a Food Handler and 8-10 hours for a Food Manager.

"**ServSafe** is a food and beverage safety[1] training and certificate program administered by the U.S. National Restaurant Association[2]. The program is accredited by ANSI[3] and the Conference for Food Protection[4].

Sanitation certification is required by most restaurants as a basic credential for their management staff. The course discusses foodborne illnesses[5], including information on specific foodborne pathogens and biological toxins, such as shellfish poisoning[6], contamination, and food allergens[7].

Prevention is also covered, with information regarding purchasing and receiving guidelines, food preparation, holding, and serving guidelines, food safety management systems, sanitation guidelines for facilities and equipment, and integrated pest control, as well as food safety regulations and employee training."[1]

Why do you need to know this? You may not be planning to work in a restaurant, but a working knowledge of food safety and practices is a great thing to have if you'll be cooking either for yourself or others. You don't want you or your guests to get sick after one of your meals, wondering what you did wrong, and avoiding you like the plague (pun intended).

Much of the bacteria that can do you in are just about unpronounceable, like vibrio parahaemolyticus, clostridium perfringens, and the all-too frequent Escherichia coli. You don't need to have a degree in microbiology to deal with this. Just follow the safe food preparation rules and you should be fine. And take comfort in the fact that most restaurants have people trained in food safety.

---

1. https://en.wikipedia.org/wiki/Food_safety

2. https://en.wikipedia.org/wiki/National_Restaurant_Association

3. https://en.wikipedia.org/wiki/ANSI

4. https://en.wikipedia.org/w/index.php?title=Conference_for_Food_Protection&action=edit&redlink=1

5. https://en.wikipedia.org/wiki/Foodborne_illness

6. https://en.wikipedia.org/wiki/Shellfish_poisoning

7. https://en.wikipedia.org/wiki/Food_allergy

A LITTLE HISTORY (paraphrased from the video cover of *The Poison Squad*):

By the close of the Industrial Revolution, the American food supply was tainted with frauds, fakes, and legions of new and untested chemicals, dangerously threatening the health of consumers. Food factories were adulterating honey with corn syrup, a slight piece of honeycomb and food dye. They were adulterating milk by stretching it with water and improving its whiteness by adding chalk and plaster of Paris. To add pretend cream, they topped it with pureed calf brains. Coffee might be largely sawdust or wheat. Pepper was often just pulverized coconut shells, charred rope, or occasionally floor sweepings. Based on the book by Deborah Blum, The Poison Squad tells the story of government chemist Dr. Harvey Wiley who, determined to banish these dangerous substances from dinner tables, took on the powerful food manufacturers and their allies. He laid the groundwork for U.S. Consumer protection laws, and ultimately the creation of the FDA.

Foodborne Illnesses:

These result from the spoilage of contaminated food, pathogenic bacteria, viruses, or parasites as well as various toxins. Symptoms may result in vomiting, diarrhea, and fever, which may set in 3 to 24 hours after ingestion. Hepatitis A—the foodborne version—symptoms may take 2 to 6 weeks to show up. What kinds of things contaminate food? It could be while it was processed or later on. It's quite a range, but here are a few:

- Chemicals
- Contaminated water
- Pesticides
- Bacteria in the soil
- Packaging materials
- Parasites occurring naturally in shellfish

Cross Contamination:

Sometimes there is nothing inherently wrong with the food, but an outside item ended up in it.

- A non-food item that was mistakenly added in the processing plant
- Hair
- Insects
- Rodent droppings
- A food that's got bacteria or salmonella contaminating another food that WAS OK before the cross contamination
- Outside of food processing, a random person could sneeze into your food and now it's contaminated—a different type of contamination, but still a bad thing

These are all issues that may have happened before you even bought the food. I don't want to inflame paranoia, though. The next time you complain about the government, be glad that there's a USDA meat inspector, shellfish regulations, health inspectors, and all kinds of laws in the U.S. where everything is inspected and documented.

———

THINGS THE COOK CAN control:

1. Keep hot food hot at 140°F or hotter.

2. Keep cold food cold at 41°F cold or colder.

3. As far as leaving food out on the counter, there is a two-hour rule for these temperatures, only one hour in the summer. If it's later than that, refrigerate! Even if the food is cooked, it does NOT negate this rule This rule also goes for groceries you just brought home.

4. Anything going in the fridge should be covered.

5. Raw meat or poultry should be contained in a bag or dish so the juices don't touch any other food, and stored down low in the fridge. Definitely discard the bag when done.

6. Raw chicken should never touch any other food and should be chopped on a separate cutting board, using a knife that doesn't touch anything else. This is how you avoid salmonella contamination. After preparing the chicken, wipe down the counter with white vinegar, which inhibits bacteria, or a sanitizer.

7. Your kitchen sink can harbor bacteria. Clean it regularly with baking soda and white vinegar.

8. Grains should be stored in airtight containers to keep out bugs. I've seen things in dried pasta that I wish I could unsee.

9. Always wash fruits and vegetables—just rinse with water—before eating. Why? The short answer is that there are different strains of bacteria in the soil. Even our grandmothers knew that.

10. The cook should wash hands frequently.

11. If the cook has long hair, he or she needs to tie hair back while cooking, not only for sanitary reasons but to keep hair from catching fire. I actually did catch my hair on fire when I was a teenager, as I leaned towards the pot cooking on a gas stove. I was OK, but the smell was awful.

12. Never put a dish towel on your shoulder where it could pick up hair. Just don't do it. If you do, my 8th grade cooking teacher, Mrs. Chew—I swear that was her name—will rise up from her grave and smite you.

13. Always keep the handles of pans turned in so dogs, children, and others don't hit them and cause a dangerous spill.

14. Never, ever store anything in the stove or the broiler drawer underneath, except for a broiler pan. A recent kitchen fire in my town illustrates this. She had parchment paper and other paper items in the drawer, turned on the oven, and it sparked a fire.

15. Be careful about kitchen curtains near a stovetop.

16. Keep a pan cover nearby in case of fire. Just put the cover on and it will smother the fire. I was forced to test this procedure recently when a candle burst into flames and I can tell you—it works immediately to put out the fire.

17. Have a fire extinguisher handy and keep it up to date. They do expire.

18. Don't buy fish from a random fish merchant. The U.S. regulates fish and shellfish and documents catches and their provenance. Buying something off of *Fish Guy with Truck You'll Never See Again* is a bad idea.

19. Remember what they say about fish and houseguests. After three days, it's time to go. Fresh fish lasts only about three days in the refrigerator, so use it by then.

20. Use a tasting spoon while cooking. Never double dip. Use the spoon once, then get another clean spoon for the next taste. None of this matters if it's just for you, but using the spoon just once is a good habit to cultivate if you will be cooking for others.

21. Keep an eye on the age of the food. There is often a "use by" date if it's unopened. But if you have leftovers, put in the container, get a piece of magic tape and write the item and the date prepared on it. For instance, "Meatballs, 12-31-2021."

22. When chopping hot peppers, avoid touching your eyes! My brother forgot this and scratched his eye inadvertently. His eye swelled up, turned red and he had a rough time of it before it subsided. You also might consider wearing disposable gloves while chopping—still not touching your eyes till you've discarded the

gloves and washed your hands.

And now a discussion of PHFs—Potentially Hazardous Foods, an actual FDA designation[2]. These are the ones that you must pay strict attention to in storage and cooking. Remember, any food at all can be cross contaminated if you're dog goes up to your perfectly prepared dish and sneezes on it, but there are other rules you must follow related to this category of foods.

POTENTIALLY HAZARDOUS FOODS

PHFs are any food that contains milk or milk products, eggs, meat, poultry, fish, shellfish, crustacean or other ingredients in a form capable of supporting rapid and progressive growth of harmful microorganisms.[3] Pay strict attention to keeping these foods at the proper temperature.

The term also applies to cut fruits and vegetables because their cut sides expose them to bacteria. The same with ground meat, since it's been cut and ground up, and if there were a problem, now it's spread throughout the meat.

Cooked potatoes are also a PHF. Cooking potatoes changes the PH (potential hydrogen) of it and now it's more open to bacteria than in its raw state.

That's probably as much science as you can stand. You'll notice that experienced cooks automatically follow the basic rules in the Things You Can Control paragraph.

GETTING STARTED

———

1. Read the recipe through first. If it says *preheat oven*, now is the time to do it. It takes 10-15 minutes, in which time you will start your recipe. That way the temperature will be correct when you finally put the food in. NOTE: If you have a convection oven—the one with the fan in the back—your food may cook about 25% faster than a regular oven.
2. Be present. Commit yourself to the recipe and don't run off in the middle of it.
3. Put on an apron. If you're like me, you'll make a mess.
4. Tie your hair back and wash your hands.
5. Assemble all your ingredients, measuring spoons and cups, pans, etc.
6. Measure all your ingredients first. This is called "Mise En Place" (pronounced Meez ? On ? Plaass). From the French, It means putting everything in place, doing all the measuring, slicing, etc. first. Professional chefs do this. You can then concentrate on the recipe without having to stop to measure something. It's more fun to work this way, like the cooking teachers on TV, although we all know some lowly assistant does the measuring ahead of time for the fancy TV chef.
7. When something says "to taste", try adding half of something, then taste or see how it looks. Add the other half if you want. You can add things, but you can't take them away if you put in too much!
8. "Divided" definition: this total amount will be used, but not all at once.
9. When shopping for ingredients for a recipe, don't be afraid to ask the supermarket people for help. They usually know what any food is and in what aisle to find it.
10. Whenever adding eggs to *any* recipe, break each egg into a separate bowl first. This way, any egg shell can be removed or if the egg is bloody (which means it was a fertilized egg), it can be discarded for a new one.
11. If you're brand new to cooking, maybe a relative or friend can stand near you (not cook, just advise) while **you** cook.

EACH RECIPE HERE WILL specify degree of difficulty. After you've gotten your feet wet with some of the easier ones, try an advanced one. You can do it!

RIDICULOUSLY EASY ★ EASY ★ MODERATELY EASY ★ ADVANCED

★

FYI:

T. means Tablespoon

t. or tsp. means teaspoon

there are 3 teaspoons in 1 Tablespoon

SUBSTITUTIONS:

Sometimes you just don't have exactly what you need in your kitchen. You can often substitute other things.

1 clove of garlic =

1 teaspoon chopped garlic

1/2 teaspoon minced garlic

1/2 teaspoon garlic flakes

1/4 teaspoon granulated garlic

1/8 teaspoon garlic powder

1 cup oil = ½ lb. butter (2 sticks)

1 T. cornstarch = 2 T. all-purpose flour

1 cup butter = 7/8 cups oil + ½ tsp. salt

1 tsp. baking powder = ½ tsp. cream of tartar + ¼ tsp. baking soda

1 square chocolate = 3 T. cocoa + 1 tsp. butter

1 cup granulated white sugar = 1 cup packed brown sugar

1 tsp. lemon juice = ½ tsp. vinegar

1 slice of bread = ½ cup bread crumbs

4 oz. cheese = 1 cup shredded cheese

1 tsp. dry herbs = 3 tsp. (or 1 T.) of fresh herbs

1 cup buttermilk = 1 cup whole milk + 1 T. vinegar

Heavy Cream = 1 cup whole milk + 1 T. melted butter

Handy Kitchen Measurements

1 Gallon	=	4 Quarts	=	16 Cups	=	8 Pints	=	3-3/4 L
1/4 Gallon	=	1 Quart	=	4 Cups	=	2 Pints	=	.94 L
1/8 Gallon	=	1/2 Quart	=	2 Cups	=	1 Pint	=	16 Fl Oz
1 Cup	=	8 Fl Oz	=	16 Tbsp	=	48 Tsp	=	237 mL
3/4 Cup	=	6 Fl Oz	=	12 Tbsp	=	36 Tsp	=	177 mL
2/3 Cup	=	5-1/3 Fl Oz	=	10-2/3 Tbsp	=	32 Tsp	=	158 mL
1/2 Cup	=	4 Fl Oz	=	8 Tbsp	=	24 Tsp	=	118 mL
1/3 Cup	=	2-2/3 Fl Oz	=	5-1/3 Tbsp	=	16 Tsp	=	79 mL
1/4 Cup	=	2 Fl Oz	=	4 Tbsp	=	12 Tsp	=	59 mL
1/8 Cup	=	1 Fl Oz	=	2 Tbsp	=	6 Tsp	=	30 mL
				1 Tbsp	=	3 Tsp	=	15 mL
						1 Tsp	=	5 mL

Source: Pinterest

APPETIZERS

CRABBIES

★ **EASY**

Don't judge this recipe from the ingredients, which look pretty lame. These are utterly delicious and look fancy when completed.

INGREDIENTS:

1 package of English muffins (6)

1 jar of Olde English Cheese (with or without pimiento)

1 stick of butter

1-1/2 tsp. mayonnaise

½ tsp. garlic salt or powder

½ tsp. seasoned salt (or use salt & pepper)

7 oz. can of crabmeat – *rinsed & drained*

DIRECTIONS:

1. In a **medium-sized mixing bowl**, blend all ingredients, except crabmeat, together till smooth.
2. Now add the crabmeat and blend well.
3. Spread on English muffins. Put in **covered storage container** with waxed paper between levels of muffins.
4. Put in the freezer for about an hour or till slightly frozen.
5. Take out of freezer and cut into quarters.
6. Bake at 450°F on UNGREASED **cookie sheet** for 8-10 minutes.

WHAT WE LEARNED:

✓ Some cooks like to rinse canned crabmeat to remove the excessive salt, then drain it so it doesn't make the recipe watery.

GUACAMOLE

★ RIDICULOUSLY EASY

This recipe is ridiculously easy. No need to spend big bucks on pre-made guac.

Don't make this unless the avocado is ripe. How to tell if your avocado is the right ripeness? Press the skin. If it gives a little, it's ready to use. Usually the skin is dark when it's the right ripeness. Once you cut it, make the recipe immediately or it will turn brown.

INGREDIENTS:

1 ripe avocado

1 T. salsa

Juice of a lime or lemon

1 T. onion - *minced fin*ely or just a shake of onion powder if you're lazy

Garlic powder to taste or none at all

DIRECTIONS:

1. Cut avocado in half, remove the pit. Scoop the flesh out with the **grapefruit spoon** I told you to buy.

   OR use an avocado tool, which scoops it out and sections it all at once.

   OR, if the avocado is really ripe, just put the avocado half face down, and pinch the skin towards you. The flesh just slips down and out.

1. In a **small mixing bowl**, mash the avocado.
2. Add other ingredients. Taste it and adjust seasoning to however you like.

NOTE: Store in an airtight container. It keeps for only a few days.

WHAT WE LEARNED:

✓ The lemon or lime juice helps to keep the avocado from turning brown.

★

<u>**NACHOS**</u> – Preheat oven to 375°F

★ **EASY**

This most excellent recipe comes from my ex-sister-in-law. At least something good came out of that relationship!

INGREDIENTS:

Nacho chips, as flat as you can find

1 can refried beans

1 jar Picante sauce or salsa

Grated cheese – Monterey jack or cheddar

DIRECTIONS:

1. Using a **cookie sheet**, lay out chips in one layer.
2. Carefully spread refried beans onto nacho chips, using a **small knife**
3. Put about 1 T. of salsa/sauce on each chip
4. Sprinkle grated cheese on top
5. Bake at 375°F till cheese is melted, about 10 minutes.

These will be soft and melty. Provide plates and napkins!

HOT ARTICHOKE DIP – Preheat oven to 350°F

★ MODERATELY EASY

There is a bit of to'ing and fro'ing between you and the food processor while making this. My late Dad loved this so much. At one of my parties, he parked himself next to the casserole and, armed with a spoon, just ate all that was left. I'm not sure he realized it was a dip . . .

This is made up of two layers—the first layer has everything *including* the artichokes. The second layer has everything *but* the artichokes. It makes for an attractive presentation. If you can find shaved Parmesan, it's even better.

INGREDIENTS:

1 can or jar (14 oz.) artichoke hearts or bottoms, *drained*

1 cup freshly grated Parmesan cheese – *divide in half*

8 ounces cream cheese, room temperature – *divide in half*

½ cup mayonnaise – *divide in half*

Garlic powder to taste

½ teaspoon dried dill

DIRECTIONS:

1. Place artichoke hearts in **food processor** and chop coarsely.
2. Add half of the remaining ingredients and process till smooth.
3. Scrape artichoke mixture into a shallow oven-proof dish, about the size of a **10" pie plate. Or use a casserole dish**.
4. Repeat procedure with remaining ingredients—the Parmesan, cream cheese, mayo, and spices—and add to mixture in the dish. Smooth top with spatula.
5. Bake at 350°F about 15 minutes. Serve immediately with breadsticks.

SAUSAGE CHEESE BALLS – Preheat oven to 375°F

★ **EASY**

I like to wear disposable gloves to make meatballs and recipes like this. Do your mise en place and chop and measure everything <u>first</u> before your hands get all messy.

INGREDIENTS:

2 packages *uncooked* roll sausage

16 oz. sharp cheddar cheese or 4 cups *shredded*

1-1/2 cups all purpose baking/biscuit mix

½ cup celery – *finely chopped*

½ onion – *finely chopped*

½ tsp. garlic powder, ½ tsp. ground thyme, ½ tsp. oregano

DIRECTIONS:

1. In a **large mixing bowl**, mix all ingredients.
2. Form into 1" balls.
3. Bake 15 minutes on **ungreased baking sheet** until golden brown.

NOTES:

- Makes about 6 dozen
- Balls can be frozen UNCOOKED. Just cook a bit longer if cooked frozen.
- For firmer texture, add extra biscuit mix and cheese

MIX-UP STUFF – Preheat oven to 250°F

★ **EASY**

INGREDIENTS:

6 T. of stick butter

2 T. Worcestershire sauce

1-1/2 tsp. seasoned salt

½ tsp. garlic powder

½ tsp. onion powder

3 cups Corn Chex™ cereal

3 cups Rice Chex™ cereal

3 cups Wheat Chex™ cereal

1 cup mixed nuts

1 cup pretzels

DIRECTIONS:

1. Melt butter in **large roasting pan** in oven.
2. Stir in seasonings.
3. Gradually stir in remaining ingredients until evenly coated.
4. Bake 1 hour, stirring every 15 minutes.
5. If microwaving, cook in microwavable bowl for 5-6 minutes on HIGH, stirring every 2 minutes.
6. Spread on paper towels to cool, then store in airtight container. Yields 12 cups

<u>SPINACH APPETIZERS</u> – Preheat oven to 350°F

★ **EASY**

INGREDIENTS:

2 packages frozen spinach – *chopped, cooked, drained*

2 cups stuffing mix

1 large onion – *chopped fine*

½ cup Parmesan

1 tsp. garlic salt

1 tsp. pepper

1 tsp. ground thyme

½ cup butter - *melted*

3 eggs - *beaten*

DIRECTIONS:

1. Do all your measuring, melting, draining, and egg beating first.
2. Now combine everything in a **large mixing bowl.**
3. Pour into a **square GREASED 8" x 8" pan**.
4. Bake at 350°F for 20 minutes till firm. Cut into squares.

PATÉ

★ EASY

NOTE: The bouillon paste, which also comes in chicken, clam base, and vegetable base, is much tastier and has less sodium than the cubes.

INGREDIENTS:

1 pound liverwurst or Braunschweiger

1 cup (8 ounces) sour cream

¼ cup green onion/scallions – *chopped*

1 tsp. beef bouillon paste

Crackers or melba toasts

DIRECTIONS:

1. In **mixer bowl**, combine all ingredients.
2. Beat until smooth.
3. Serve with any kind of crackers you like.
4. Refrigerate leftovers.

★

ZUCCHINI PUFFS – Stovetop

★ MODERATELY EASY

There's a joke at harvest time in New England that people only lock their cars so neighbors won't throw the ubiquitous zucchini in it. This will use up some of it, at least, and it's delicious. You fry them like pancakes.

INGREDIENTS:

2 medium-sized zucchini - *grated*

2 large eggs

1-1/2 cups flour

¼ cup vegetable oil

2-1/2 teaspoons baking powder

Fresh parsley – *chop off the stems*

Grated Parmesan

Garlic powder, salt and pepper to taste

DIRECTIONS:

1. Wash and dry zucchini. Grate with skin on and set aside in a **small bowl**.
2. In a **large bowl**, beat eggs, salt, pepper, garlic powder, grated cheese, and parsley.
3. Mix flour together with zucchini in the small bowl.
4. Add flour mixture slowly to egg mixture. Blend thoroughly.
5. Heat **non-stick skillet** for 60 seconds. Add vegetable oil and heat another 60 seconds.
6. Spoon mixture into pancake sized medallions into hot oil.
7. Cook till brown on both sides, attending carefully (DON'T WALK AWAY!), and flipping with a **non-stick flipper**. Drain on paper towels.

BEVERAGES

IF YOU DON'T HAVE A fancy crystal punch bowl, don't worry. Just get a large plastic bowl at the dollar store, some paper cups, and a ladle.

This chapter also has a recipe for homemade hot cocoa, which will make your forget those packets you've been using.

SPICY FRUIT PUNCH – make the syrup several hours before your party. This is particularly nice at Christmas.

★ **MODERATELY EASY**

INGREDIENTS:

1 cup sugar

1 cup water

1-1/2 tsp. ground cinnamon

½ tsp. ground cloves

Two 46-oz. cans Hawaiian Punch Fruit Juicy-Red®, chilled*

One 32 oz. bottle cranberry-apple drink

Citrus slices for garnish – optional

Ice cubes

*If Hawaiian Punch® is too sweet, substitute 11 cups of your choice of fruit juice—pineapple, apple, etc.

DIRECTIONS:

1. In a **small saucepan**, mix sugar, water, and spices. Bring to a boil.
2. Cover and simmer gently 10 minutes. It will make a syrup.
3. Refrigerate until chilled.
4. When ready to serve, mix the syrup with Hawaiian Punch® and cran-apple drink in **punch bowl**.
5. Garnish with citrus slices, add ice. YIELD: about 32 four-ounce servings.

OCEAN-SPRAY HOLIDAY PUNCH WITH HOLIDAY RING

★ ADVANCED

The day before your party, make the ring. This makes a nice presentation.

INGREDIENTS:

One lemon – *sliced, seeds removed*

One lime – *sliced, seeds removed*

Two 64 oz. cartons of Ocean Spray Crantastic® or Cran-Orange®

2-liter bottle of lemon-lime soda

1 bottle (750 ml – standard size) of white wine (optional)

2 more lemons – *squeeze juice*

2 more limes – *squeeze juice*

DIRECTIONS:

1. Cut one lemon and one lime into thin slices, remove seeds. Arrange alternating slices in the bottom of a **3-1/2 cup ring mold**. If you don't have a mold, you can use anything round, preferably with a cover.
2. Pour in enough cranberry juice to barely cover fruit. Freeze until JUST set.
3. Now add enough cranberry juice to fill the mold. Freeze OVERNIGHT.
4. Just before serving, make the punch. Squeeze juice from the 2 other lemons & limes. In a **large punch bowl**, mix citrus juice with remaining fruit juice, soda, and wine. Stir gently.
5. Unmold frozen ring and float in the punch. If it looks too stubborn to release, immerse <u>bottom</u> of mold in sink full of hot water for just 10 seconds or so.
6. YIELD: 35 six-oz. servings.

LEMONBERRY PUNCH

★ **EASY**

NOTE: If this is too sweet, you can always substitute with low-sugar items.

INGREDIENTS:

4 scoops of dry lemonade mix

4 cups water

½ cup cranberry juice

1-1/2 cups lemon-lime soda

Ice cubes

DIRECTIONS:

1. Mix all in a giant punch bowl or pitcher. Add ice cubes.
2. YIELD: 1-1/2 quarts

HOMEMADE HOT COCOA

★ MODERATELY EASY

TIP: Anything with sugar or chocolate in it can become super hot and burn easily. Once you burn chocolate, it's no good, so stay with this until it's done.

INGREDIENTS:

- 1.5 oz of good quality dark chocolate (½ a bar)
- 1 teaspoon unsweetened cocoa, high quality like Lake Champlain
- 8 oz Milk

DIRECTIONS:

1. Chop chocolate bar finely.

2. In a **small saucepan** combine the dark chocolate, cocoa powder, and milk.

3. Heat over LOW heat, stirring constantly with a **whisk** to prevent the chocolate from settling.

4. Once all of the chocolate is well blended, slightly **raise** the heat to MEDIUM. DO NOT WALK AWAY. Stir frequently until you see the steam and bubbles appearing at the edge, to about 120°F, then take off heat immediately.

OPTIONS:

- Try different types of chocolate bar, such as milk chocolate
- Spike with bourbon, brandy, or Irish Whisky
- Add more unsweetened cocoa if desired
- Try adding espresso syrup or espresso powder for a mocha drink

★

BREADS & MUFFINS

FRITTATA – Preheat oven to 350°F

★ EASY

INGREDIENTS:

1 tsp. olive oil

1-1/2 cups baby spinach - *sautéed*

1 garlic clove – *minced* OR ¼ tsp. garlic powder

4 slices prosciutto – *cooked and diced*

¼ cup onions – *sautéed*

4 eggs

2-1/2 T. whole milk or cream

1/8 tsp. salt

1/8 tsp. ground black pepper

1 T. fresh chives – chopped/snipped

2 oz. cheese – *shredded* (I like Gruyere, Swiss, or cheddar)

DIRECTIONS:

1. In **medium-sized skillet**, sauté spinach in 1 tsp. olive oil (with garlic if used). This only takes a few minutes. Remove from pan and set aside.
2. In the **same skillet**, sauté onion and prosciutto about 5 minutes
3. In a **large mixing bowl**, mix eggs, cream, salt & pepper, and chives.
4. **Butter or oil a casserole, pie pan, or cast iron skillet** (not with spray). Lay in the sautéed veggies and sprinkle the cheese over them.
5. Pour in the egg mixture over all.
6. Bake at 350°F about 8 to 20 minutes or until center jiggles just a bit. It will continue to cook a little when you take it out of the oven.

WHAT WE LEARNED:

✓ Cook veggies first or they'll make your frittata watery.

✓ Spinach cooks really fast and will reduce its volume significantly. You'll see.

✓ Try with other veggies like mushrooms, zucchini, etc. Sauté first!

★

HONEY PUFF PANCAKE – Preheat oven to 400°F. Use blender. Serves 4

★ **MODERATELY EASY**

INGREDIENTS:

1 cup milk

6 eggs

3 T. honey

3 oz. cream cheese

1 cup flour

½ tsp. salt

½ tsp. baking powder

3 T. butter

GARNISH: Confectioner's sugar, jelly, lemon wedges

DIRECTIONS:

1. Lightly spoon flour into measuring cup; level off. In **blender**, place all ingredients except garnish; let stand while greasing **oven-proof skillet or au gratin pan**.
2. Grease pan with 1 T. butter. Add remaining 2 T. butter to pan; heat in oven 2 minutes.
3. While pan is in oven, blend ingredients at high speed 1 minute or until smooth.
4. Remove skillet from oven and *immediately* pour batter into hot pan. Bake about 20 minutes or till puffed and dark golden brown.
5. Serve immediately with powdered sugar, jelly and a lemon wedge.

WHAT WE LEARNED:

✓ How to measure flour—lightly, not packed.

✓ Pouring batter into a hot pan is what makes the final product puffy, the same technique used in making popovers.

KATHY'S CRISP WAFFLES – waffle iron and oven

★ **EASY**

My best friend used to serve these when she owned a bed & breakfast in Vermont.

INGREDIENTS:

2 eggs

1-3/4 cups milk

½ cup (1 stick) butter OR vegetable oil

2 cups flour

4 tsp. baking powder

1 T. sugar

OPTIONAL TOPPING: Fresh or frozen strawberries. Add sugar to taste and let set for an hour or overnight. It makes its own sauce. Top with whipped cream.

DIRECTIONS:

1. Grease (using solid shortening) and preheat **waffle iron**. Heat oven to 200°F to keep completed waffles warm.
2. In a **large mixing bowl**, beat eggs till fluffy.
3. Beat in remaining ingredients just until smooth.
4. Put enough batter onto waffle iron to fill the grooves without overfilling.
5. Cook about 2-1/2 to 3 minutes per waffle. While the waffles are cooking, set the table, and heat up some maple syrup.
6. YIELD: 6 waffles

WHAT WE LEARNED:

✓ How to coordinate waffle making, ensuring that they're not overdone, and keeping them warm till serving time.

✓ How to make strawberry sauce.

★

BLUEBERRY MUFFINS – Preheat oven to 375°F

★ MODERATELY EASY

INGREDIENTS:

½ cup (1 stick) butter

2 eggs

½ cup milk

1-1/4 cup sugar

2 cups flour

½ tsp. salt

2 tsp. baking powder

2-1/2 cups blueberries OR cranberries OR 2 bananas

DIRECTIONS:

1. In a **large bowl**, cream butter (just mash it up) and add eggs one at a time.
2. Add milk.
3. Sift dry ingredients in **small separate bowl**. Now add to large bowl.
4. Mash 1 cup blueberries. Add with remaining blueberries to mixture and stir by hand ONLY TILL MOISTENED. Don't overstir.
5. GREASE **12-cup muffin tin** inside and on top OR use paper liners.
6. Fill to the top with batter. Sprinkle sugar on top.
7. Bake at 375°F 25-30 minutes, or until a toothpick inserted in the middle comes out clean. If it has batter on it or crumbs, bake for a few more minutes.

WHAT WE LEARNED:

✓ Whenever adding eggs to *any* recipe, break each egg into a separate bowl first. This way, any egg shell can be removed or if the egg is bloody, it can be discarded for a new one.

✓ Muffins are always made with wet ingredients in one bowl, dry ingredients in another bowl, then put together and stirred just till mixed. Overmixing makes muffins tough.

✓ How to test for doneness. The tester or toothpick should not come out with batter on it.

★

POPPY SEED MUFFINS – Preheat oven to 375°F.

★ **MODERATELY EASY**

INGREDIENTS:

2 cups flour

¼ cup poppy seeds

½ tsp. salt

¼ tsp. baking soda

½ cup butter (1 stick) – *room temperature*

¾ cup sugar

2 eggs

¾ cup sour cream

1-1/2 tsp. vanilla

DIRECTIONS:

1. Preheat oven to 375°. GREASE one **12-cup muffin tin** OR use paper liners.
2. Combine flour, poppy seeds, salt, and baking soda in **small bowl**.
3. In **large electric mixer bowl**, cream butter with sugar till light.
4. Beat in eggs, one at a time.
5. Blend in sour cream and vanilla.
6. Gradually beat in dry ingredients just till mixed.
7. Bake until tester inserted in centers comes out clean, about 20 minutes.
8. Cool 5 minutes on rack while still in muffin tin, then remove from tin.

NOTES:

✓ Beating this muffin batter with an electric mixer contradicts the blueberry muffin recipe instruction to mix by hand. All I know is it still comes out great.

✓ Don't eat poppy seeds if you're expecting a drug test. It will give a false positive.

✓ *Gradually* beating in dry ingredients will ensure that you don't get a face full of flour.

CRANBERRY-ORANGE NUT BREAD – Preheat oven to 350°F

★ **MODERATELY EASY**

INGREDIENTS:

2 cups flour

1 cup sugar

1-1/2 tsp. baking powder

½ tsp. baking soda

1 tsp. salt

¼ cup solid shortening

¾ cup orange juice

1 T. grated orange rind OR 1 T. concentrated orange juice

1 egg – *well beaten*

½ cup nuts - *chopped*

1 cup cranberries – *halved*

DIRECTIONS:

1. Sift together dry ingredients in a **large bowl**.
2. Cut in shortening, using a **pastry blender** or large fork.
3. Mix orange juice & rind and beaten egg in **small separate bowl**.
4. Pour into dry ingredients. Mix just enough to dampen. Don't overmix.
5. Fold in nuts and cranberries.
6. Spoon batter into GREASED **loaf pan (9" x 5" x 3")**, spreading into corners and sides slightly higher than center.
7. Bake at 350°F 1 hour or until crust is golden brown or till toothpick comes out clean. Slices better second day. Delicious with cream cheese.

GRETA'S CORN BREAD – Preheat oven to 350°F

★ EASY

INGREDIENTS:

2 boxes Jiffy® Cornbread Mix

8 oz. sour cream

2 eggs – *beaten*

1 can niblets corn - *drained*

1 can creamed corn

1 stick butter - *melted*

DIRECTIONS:

1. GREASE **13" x 9" pan** with butter.
2. In a **large mixing bowl**, mix eggs, corn, and sour cream.
3. Now add cornbread mix and the melted butter. Pour into prepared pan.
4. Bake at 350°F for 35-40 minutes.

NOTE: Serve this fresh out of the oven and refrigerate any leftovers. It keeps for only a few days.

OPTIONS: Add cheddar cheese or mild jalapeños for a Mexican accent.

<u>OATMEAL DATENUT BREAD</u> – Preheat oven to 350°F

★ **EASY**

INGREDIENTS:

2 eggs - *beaten*

1 cup sugar

2 cups buttermilk

2/3 cup molasses

3 cups flour

2 tsp. baking soda

1 tsp. baking powder

1 tsp. salt

1-1/2 cups oatmeal

1-1/2 cups pecans or walnuts – *chopped*

1-1/2 cups dates – *chopped*

DIRECTIONS:

1. Preheat oven to 350°F. GREASE **2 small loaf pans** with shortening or butter.
2. Mix all ingredients in a **large bowl**.
3. Pour into two loaf pans or whatever fits. Bake at 350°F for 50-60 minutes.

<u>PUMPKIN BREAD</u> – Preheat oven to 350°F.

★ **EASY**

INGREDIENTS:

4 cups sugar

4 eggs - *beaten*

1 cup vegetable or canola oil

1 can pumpkin (for pies)

3-1/2 cups flour

2 tsp. baking powder

2 tsp. baking soda

2 tsp. salt

Pinch nutmeg

½ tsp. ground cinnamon

½ tsp. ground cloves

DIRECTIONS:

1. Preheat oven to 350°F. GREASE and flour **2 medium loaf pans or 3 small**.
2. By hand, blend all ingredients in **large mixing bowl**. Pour into pans.
3. Bake 1 hour at 350°F.

WHAT WE LEARNED:

✓ To grease and flour a pan: grease first with solid shortening. Put 1 tablespoon of flour into pan. Because it gets messy, do this over a wastebasket. Tip it all around until it covers the grease. This keeps the cake or bread from sticking.

PARMESAN BREADSTICK CANDY CANES – Preheat oven to 350°F

★ MODERATELY EASY

INGREDIENTS:

One 11 oz. can refrigerated soft breadsticks

3 T. butter – *melted*

¾ cup grated Parmesan

DIRECTIONS:

1. Preheat oven to 350°F. Set out **2 shallow bowls**.
2. Cut breadsticks in half to make 16.
3. In one bowl, put melted butter. Dip breadsticks.
4. In another bowl, put parmesan cheese. Dip buttered breadsticks in cheese.
5. Twist and shape into candy canes on UNGREASED **cookie sheet**.
6. Bake at 350°F for 14-18 minutes or until golden brown.

NOTE: These are a big hit at Christmas and a more interesting offering than the typical dinner rolls.

<u>MRS. HUMPHRIES SCONES</u> – Preheat oven to 425°F

★ MODERATELY EASY

Scones can be dry, but these are moist inside and crispy outside. Mrs. Humphries was an elderly English woman with a connection to the King Arthur Flour company, so you know this recipe is authentic. It calls for the cook to make an executive decision about the dough. Do your best, make notes, and enjoy!

INGREDIENTS:

1 cup flour

½ cup sugar

2 tsp. baking powder

3 T. butter

½ cup raisins or crannies (if you leave them out, it won't matter)

1 egg – *beaten*

½ tsp. lemon extract

Less than ¼ cup of milk

Sugar to sprinkle on top (optional)

DIRECTIONS:

1. In a **large mixing bowl** combine flour, sugar, and baking powder.
2. Add butter and mix with a **pastry blender** or fork.
3. Now add raisins, beaten egg, and lemon extract. Mush it up.
4. Add just enough milk to make the dough soft but not too sticky.
5. Drop big tablespoons of batter onto a GREASED **cookie sheet**.
6. Sprinkle with sugar if desired.
7. Bake at 425°F for 12-15 minutes. Serve immediately.

WHAT WE LEARNED:

✓ How to work with dough for drop biscuits/scones

CASSEROLES

SAUSAGE, POTATO, & VEGETABLE CASSEROLE – Preheat oven to 350°F

★ EASY

INGREDIENTS:

1 cup frozen shredded hash brown potatoes

½ cup frozen corn kernels

½ cup frozen green pepper strips – *thawed* OR fresh

2 T. pimiento – *drained and chopped*

4 oz. turkey sausage – UNCOOKED – *thinly sliced*

½ cup skim milk

1 large egg

1/8 tsp. salt and pepper

1/8 tsp. ground thyme

½ tsp. onion powder

½ cup shredded cheese

DIRECTIONS:

1. Coat a **medium square or rectangular baking dish** with no-stick cooking spray
2. Place hash browns in dish. Top with corn and peppers, then sausage.
3. In a **small bowl**, beat milk, egg, salt & pepper.
4. Pour over items in dish.
5. Bake at 350°F for 25 minutes, take out of oven and sprinkle on cheese.
6. Bake another 5 minutes. Serves 2.

WHAT WE LEARNED:

✓ That cheese should often be put on near the end of baking. Otherwise, the cheese will overcook.

✓ Items from the freezer can be put together easily to produce a homemade dish.

CAJUN CASSEROLE – Preheat oven to 350°F

★ MODERATELY EASY

This recipe does have a lot of ingredients and a bit of running around the kitchen. But it is just too delicious to leave out. See if you can get someone else to wash the dishes.

INGREDIENTS:

One 8 oz. package of cream cheese – *cubed*

4 T. butter – *divided*

1 large onion – *chopped*

2 celery ribs – *chopped*

1 large green pepper – *chopped* OR 4.5 oz. can of chilies

1 pound COOKED medium shrimp

2 cans (6 oz.) crabmeat – *rinsed and drained*

1 can cream of mushroom soup

¾ cup COOKED rice

1 jar (4.5 oz.) sliced mushrooms – *drained*

1 tsp. garlic salt or powder

½ tsp. cayenne pepper OR Cajun seasoning (I like Tony Chachere's)

¾ cup cheddar cheese - *shredded*

½ cup (12) Ritz® crackers – *crushed* - with 1 T. butter

DIRECTIONS:

1. Measure and chop all ingredients first.
2. In **small saucepan**, cook and stir cream cheese and 2 T. butter over low heat until melted and smooth.
3. In a **large cast iron or ovenproof skillet** sauté onion, celery, and green pepper in remaining 2 T. butter till tender, 6 to 8 minutes.
4. Stir in shrimp, crab, mushroom soup, rice, mushrooms, seasonings, and cream cheese mixture.
5. TOPPING: Combine cracker crumbs with cheese and 1 T. melted butter.
6. Bake UNCOVERED in 350°F oven till bubbly, about 25 minutes. Serves 8.

WHAT WE LEARNED:

✓ Onion, celery, and bell pepper is called the "holy trinity" or mirepoix by Cajuns. It is used in many of their recipes. It can be found in the supermarket, chopped up and ready for use.

✓ Divided – means you will use this amount in several stages, not all at once.

CHERYL'S CHICKEN STUFFING CASSEROLE – Preheat oven to 325°F

★ MODERATELY EASY

I called it moderately easy, not because it's complicated. It's because it will take you a while to dice the cooked chicken. You can always do this in stages. Cook the chicken one day, cool it properly, and dice the next day. This recipe is from my sister-in-law, who is an awesome cook.

INGREDIENTS:

5 whole chicken breasts – *boneless*

1 T. chicken bouillon paste

1 cup cream mushroom soup

2 cups fresh sliced mushrooms - *sauté*

1 pint sour cream

1 package Pepperidge Farm® stuffing } *Mix together for topping*

1 stick butter – *melted }*

1 cup chicken broth }

DIRECTIONS:

1. BUTTER a **13" x 9" pan** (unless planning to bake the next day).
2. Put chicken in a **deep stockpot** with water to cover. Boil chicken with bouillon paste till no longer pink. Check after 15 minutes. **Save the broth!**
3. Cool 30 minutes on counter, stirring occasionally, then refrigerate, covered. This relates to food safety.
4. Dice cooled chicken.
5. In **large mixing bowl**, mix diced chicken, sautéed mushrooms, and sour cream. Pour into prepared pan. Put on topping.
6. Bake at 325°F for 45 minutes. Serves 8.
7. Save remaining broth to make soup. Put in freezer if you can't deal with it now.

WHAT WE LEARNED:

✓ How to do a laborious recipe in stages.

✓ How to cook chicken, ensuring its proper doneness.

✓ How to plan to use other parts of the recipe for future use.

★

VINNIE'S IMPOSSIBLE TURKEY PIE – Preheat oven to 400°F

★ **MODERATELY EASY**

INGREDIENTS:

2 cups COOKED turkey – *diced*

1 jar or can (4.5 oz.) sliced mushrooms OR ½ cup sliced fresh mushrooms – *sautéed*

½ cup scallions – *diced, using scissors*

½ tsp. salt

1 cup Swiss cheese – *shredded*

1-1/2 cups milk

¾ cup Bisquick® baking mix

3 eggs

———————————

DIRECTIONS:

1. Preheat over to 400°F. GREASE a **10" pie plate**.
2. Sprinkle turkey, mushrooms, scallions, salt, and cheese in bottom of plate.
3. In **blender**, beat milk, baking mix, and eggs until smooth, about 15 seconds on HIGH.
4. Pour over ingredients in pie plate.
5. Bake at 400°F until knife inserted between center and edge comes out clean, about 30-35 minutes. Cool 5 minutes.

———————————

WHAT WE LEARNED:

✓ Slice scallions with herb cutters (little scissors) or regular scissors as opposed to chopping them. It's much faster.

✓ Blending the batter on high incorporates air into it and makes a nice light, puffy end product.

✓ Testing this quiche-like dish for doneness. Inserting knife between center and edge ensures that it's cooked, as the center tends to cook last.

AUNT RUTH'S BAKED EGGS & CHEESE – Preheat oven to 325°F.

★ EASY

Another great recipe from my friend Kathy, who used to make this when she owned a bed & breakfast in Vermont. You just dump everything in together.

————————

INGREDIENTS:

7 eggs

1 cup milk

2 teaspoons sugar

1 lb. Monterey jack cheese – *shredded*

4 oz. cream cheese – *cubed*

16 oz. cottage cheese

6 T. butter – *cubed*

½ cup flour

1 tsp. baking powder

DIRECTIONS:

1. In **large bowl**, beat together eggs, milk, and sugar.
2. Add cheeses, butter, flour, and baking powder. Mix well.
3. Pour in **13" x 9" glass baking dish**, UNGREASED.
4. Bake at 325°F for 45 minutes or until knife inserted in center comes out clean.
5. If made ahead and refrigerated, bake for 60 minutes. SERVES 8.

VARIATIONS: Chive cottage cheese, low-fat cheeses, mushrooms, zucchini

WHAT WE LEARNED:

✓ How to make a one-dish meal for brunch or company staying overnight.

<u>**MOUSSAKA**</u> – Preheat oven to 350°F

★ **ADVANCED**

Okay, I lied. Every recipe in this book is not easy. This one has layers of activity and dirties every pan in the house. But . . . do you like Moussaka? Good luck finding it on a menu. So you must boldly go where you've not gone before and make it yourself. I've tweaked this recipe for maximum deliciousness. Some day you'll thank me.

INGREDIENTS:

1 eggplant

2 T. butter

1 lb. ground lamb OR ground beef OR ground chicken

1 to 2 onions (you decide) – *chopped*

½ tsp. thyme

½ tsp. oregano

½ cup wine (any kind)

<u>1 cup of canned tomatoes OR tomato sauce</u>

8 T. fine dry bread crumbs - *divided*

2 eggs – *separated. How?* Get out 2 small bowls. Crack the egg carefully, holding it vertically and separating shell into two halves. Go back and forth between halves, letting the whites fall into one bowl. Put yolks into the other bowl.

Olive oil for drizzling

2 cups béchamel sauce – see separate recipe

MOUSSAKA DIRECTIONS:

1. Make béchamel sauce first and cool in refrigerator – see separate recipe.
2. Slice eggplant into equal sized round slices and cook in a **large casserole** in microwave 6 minutes at 70%. When done, put a heavy plate on top of eggplant; then put a heavy pan or hamburger press on top of plate. It drains excess water out of the eggplant. For this recipe you can use them whole or grind them in the food processor.
3. Preheat oven to 350°F. GREASE a **13" x 9" pan**.
4. In **large skillet**, cook meat until lightly browned. Add 2 T. butter, onion and seasonings; cook till onion is soft.
5. Add wine and tomatoes/sauce. Simmer 10 minutes. Take off heat.
6. Stir in 4 T. of the bread crumbs and 2 egg whites. Mix well.
7. Spread 2 T. of crumbs in bottom of 13"x 9" pan. Layer eggplant, meat mixture, eggplant, meat mixture (usually 2 layers).
8. Beat the 2 egg yolks into béchamel sauce. Pour over casserole. Top with remaining 2 T. of crumbs. Drizzle with olive oil.
9. Bake at 350°F for 45-60 minutes or till heated through. There will be a nice crust on top. SERVES 8

WHAT WE LEARNED:

✓ How to cook eggplant and drain. (You can also fry it if desired.)

✓ How to separate an egg

✓ Why take off heat before adding egg? So you don't have scrambled egg in the dish. Eggs are used here as a thickening agent.

✓ How to stick with a complicated recipe. This will take about 45 minutes to put together.

<u>BECHAMEL SAUCE FOR MOUSSAKA</u> - Stovetop

★ MODERATELY EASY

This is the topping for moussaka but can be used in other recipes as well, like mac n' cheese, lasagna, or just pour over whatever you like. You start with making a roux (/roo/) a mixture of flour and fat—another cooking lesson for you.

INGREDIENTS:

4 T. butter

6 T. flour

2 cups milk – *hot (2 minutes in microwave)*

½ tsp. salt

½ tsp. pepper

½ tsp. nutmeg or more – this is what gives it that unique taste.

DIRECTIONS:

1. Melt butter in **3-quart heavy saucepan**. Add flour and cook on MEDIUM HEAT, stirring constantly with **whisk** for 2 minutes or until roux is smooth and begins to bubble. DO NOT ALLOW TO BURN!
2. Remove saucepan from heat. Add hot milk all at once.
3. Return pan to heat. Stir vigorously with a whisk and continue cooking on MEDIUM HEAT. Sauce will be thick and smooth within about 1 minute.
4. Add seasonings. Taste. Add more if you wish. Now continue to cook over VERY LOW HEAT about 10 minutes. YIELD: 2 cups.

WHAT WE LEARNED:

✓ How to make a roux (used in so many recipes!)

✓ How to cook a sauce to its desired thickness

★

SALADS

GREEK SALAD

★ **EASY**

Inspired by a restaurant in my hometown owned by a Greek immigrant, who made the best salads. Simple, savory, and just the thing for a hot day.

INGREDIENTS:

Iceberg lettuce

Tomatoes – *quartered*

Feta cheese

Kalamata olives

Red onion – *sliced*

Yasou® Greek salad dressing

DIRECTIONS:

1. Wash lettuce, pat dry (unless using pre-washed lettuce).
2. In a **large bowl**, combine lettuce and tomatoes. Toss with Yasou® dressing, or try my Greek Dressing in my Salad Dressings & More chapter.
3. Top with Feta cheese, a few Kalamata olives, and red onion.

WHAT WE LEARNED:

✓ That you must wash lettuce and dry before using. The dressing will stick to the dried lettuce better than if you leave it wet.

✓ Let your guests know if the olives have been pitted. If not, remind them.

✓ This recipe depends on how many people will be eating it, so there are no measurements. Also, there is room for interpretation. If you don't like onion, leave it out. If you like pepperoncini or banana peppers, add them.

★

ARUGULA, APPLE & GOAT CHEESE SALAD

★ **MODERATELY EASY**

SALAD INGREDIENTS:

2 apples – *cored, peeled, sliced*

½ cup pecan halves – candied or not

8 cups baby arugula lettuce

4 oz. goat cheese – *crumbled*

¼ cup scallions – *cut with scissors*

DRESSING:

2 T. apple cider – or any sweet juice

2 T. oil – olive or avocado oil

1 T. apple cider vinegar – or Balsamic

2 tsp. Dijon mustard

DIRECTIONS:

1. In **small pitcher**, mix the dressing with wire **whisk**.
2. Peel, core, and slice apples.
3. Arrange lettuce, pecans, apples, goat cheese, and scallions on individual plates.
4. Serve dressing on the side. Serves 6.

WHAT WE LEARNED:

✓ How to mix sweet and salty for a sophisticated salad.

✓ That cutting scallions with scissors is easier than chopping with a knife.

✓ How easy it is to make your own dressing.

SPINACH SALAD

★ **EASY**

This looks pretty and is a nice contrast to the usual garden salad.

SALAD INGREDIENTS:

4 cups raw spinach

1 can (11 oz.) mandarin oranges - *drained*

1 cup fresh mushrooms – *sliced*

¾ cup walnuts

½ cup red onion – sliced

DRESSING:

¼ cup olive oil

¼ cup rice wine vinegar

2 T. orange juice

2 T. honey

DIRECTIONS:

1. Wash spinach, pat dry.
2. In **small pitcher**, make dressing and mix with wire **whisk**.
3. Combine salad ingredients.
4. Serve dressing on the side or dress entire salad.

CUCUMBER SALAD

★ **EASY**

INGREDIENTS:

2 English cucumbers – *sliced thin*

1 T. salt

1 small white onion – *sliced thin*

1 cup white vinegar

½ cup water

¾ cup white granulated sugar

1 T. dried dill – or to taste

DIRECTIONS:

1. Sprinkle the 1 T. of salt over sliced cucumbers. Cover for 2 hours. Pour off excess liquid and pat dry.
2. Toss cukes and onion in **large bowl**.
3. In **medium-sized saucepan**, combine vinegar, water, and sugar over MEDIUM-HIGH HEAT. Bring to a boil, then remove from heat.
4. Pour over the cukes.
5. Stir in the dill.
6. Cover and refrigerate till cold, at least 1 hour.

WHAT WE LEARNED:

✓ That salt draws excess liquid out of a vegetable, keeping it from getting soggy. This method is also used with eggplant and will reduce bitterness.

✓ English cucumbers are seedless and a bit sweeter than regular cucumbers, thus they are ideal for this recipe.

MACARONI SALAD

★ MODERATELY EASY

There's an overnight component, but taste it and you'll agree it's worth waiting for.

INGREDIENTS:

4 cups elbow macaroni – uncooked (1 box)

SAUCE:

1 cup mayonnaise

¼ cup white vinegar

¼ to ¾ cup sugar – your preference

2-1/2 tsp. mustard

1-1/2 tsp. salt

½ tsp. black pepper

1 onion – *chopped fine*

1 green pepper – *diced*

2 stalks celery – *diced*

2 T. pimiento

DIRECTIONS:

1. Boil elbows according to package directions. Drain.
2. Rinse with cool water, then rinse with 2 T. of the vinegar. Cool.
3. In **medium-sized mixing bowl**, make sauce. Pour <u>half</u> over cooled, cooked elbows. Refrigerate overnight. Refrigerate other half of sauce for later.
4. Next day, pour remainder of sauce on.

WHAT WE LEARNED:

✓ Allowing the sauce to permeate the macaroni overnight in the fridge allows the flavors to meld together.

✓ Patience and planning ahead with overnight-required directions.

POTATO SALAD VINAIGRETTE - stovetop

★ EASY

Here is a great recipe for a hot summer day. The vinegar inhibits bacterial growth better than mayonnaise, so it's just the thing for a picnic.

INGREDIENTS:

3 pounds red new potatoes - whole

¼ cup red wine vinegar

3 T. whole grain prepared Dijon mustard

½ cup olive oil

6 scallions – *cut with scissors*

½ cup fresh parsley – *chopped*

¼ cup fresh dill – *chopped* OR 1 T. dried dill or to taste

1-2 T. sweet pickle juice

DIRECTIONS:

1. Put potatoes in **large pot** of COLD salted water to cover potatoes. BRING TO A BOIL, THEN LOWER TO SIMMER; cook till fork tender, about 15 minutes.
2. Drain in a **colander** and allow to cool, about 30 minutes. When cooled, cut potatoes in half.
3. Combine vinegar and mustard in a **large bowl**. Slowly whisk in olive oil.
4. Add potatoes to the vinaigrette, and mix gently but thoroughly.
5. Toss in scallions, parsley, sweet pickle juice, and dill. Salt & pepper to taste.

WHAT WE LEARNED:

✓ Red new potatoes and cooking them whole absorbs less water than white, cut-up baking potatoes. This is more important for a recipe like this.

SALAD DRESSINGS & MORE

CELERY SEED DRESSING - blender

★ EASY

This is a sweet and elegant dressing that is also good on pasta salad.

INGREDIENTS:

1 cup Extra Virgin Olive Oil

¼ cup sugar

1 tsp. dry mustard powder

⅛ cup onion – *chopped fine*

¼ cup vinegar

½ tsp. celery seed

DIRECTIONS:

1. Blend all ingredients in **blender** until thoroughly mixed.
2. Refrigerate.
3. Take out 30 minutes before serving.

WHAT WE LEARNED:

✓ That when you put oil and vinegar together, it needs to be mixed thoroughly or it will separate.

GREEK DRESSING - blender

★ **EASY**

INGREDIENTS:

2 cloves garlic – *minced* OR ½ tsp. garlic powder

1-1/2 tsp. Dijon mustard

½ cup Extra Virgin Olive Oil

2 T. lemon juice

½ tsp. sugar

5 T. Red wine vinegar

½ tsp. dried basil

¼ tsp. dried oregano

DIRECTIONS:

1. Put all except olive oil in **blender**.
2. Pulse several times.
3. With blender running on HIGH, slowly pour olive oil through lid insert in top of blender until dressing is creamy. Refrigerate.

★

CAESAR DRESSING – blender or immersion blender

★ **EASY**

INGREDIENTS:

2 anchovy fillets OR 1 tsp. anchovy paste

2 cloves garlic OR ½ tsp. garlic powder

1 cup mayonnaise

¼ cup vinegar

1/3 cup grated Parmesan

2 T. lemon juice

1 T. Dijon mustard

2 tsp. Worcestershire sauce

DIRECTIONS:

1. Combine anchovies and garlic.
2. Process remaining ingredients in **blender** till smooth.
3. If using an **immersion blender**, blend all in a **glass measuring cup**.
4. YIELD: ½ to ¾ cup of dressing, usually served over Romaine lettuce.

WHAT WE LEARNED:

✓ In the olden days (1970s) chefs used to coat the romaine lettuce leaves with a raw, beaten egg yolk to make grated Parmesan stick to the leaves when making a Caesar salad. We usually don't use raw egg any longer today, as they can be a source of salmonella. There is a method of microwaving the egg with lemon juice to make it safe, but do you really want to bother? Coating romaine with a bit of olive oil or avocado oil achieves the same thing safely.

BLUE CHEESE DRESSING – mix by hand

★ **EASY**

INGREDIENTS:

4 oz. blue cheese - *crumbled*

1 cup mayonnaise

1 cup heavy cream

1 clove garlic – minced OR ½ tsp. garlic powder

2 T. red wine vinegar

½ tsp. salt

¼ tsp. ground black pepper

DIRECTIONS:

1. In **medium-sized mixing bowl**, put all ingredients except blue cheese. Mix thoroughly with wire **whisk**.
2. Now add crumbled blue cheese and mix thoroughly.
3. Refrigerate 1 hour to meld flavors together.

<u>WHOPPER SAUCE</u> – mix by hand

★ **EASY**

Offer this to your guests for their burgers at your next cookout and be a star.

INGREDIENTS:

½ cup mayonnaise

½ cup sour cream

¼ cup ketchup

1 tsp. Worcestershire sauce

1/8 tsp. horseradish sauce (see What We Learned, below)

1/8 cup onion – *minced*

¼ tsp. cayenne pepper

DIRECTIONS:

1. In **medium-sized mixing bowl**, mix all ingredients well, using a **whisk**. Refrigerate.

WHAT WE LEARNED:

✓ Horseradish is extremely strong. A little goes a long way unless you really need your sinuses cleared out. My husband, a retired safety inspector for an insurance company, once visited a horseradish factory where the Mixing Room was equipped with an aircraft-sized fan to exhaust the pungent fumes, and still they issued him an industrial-strength respirator (not a dust mask!) to survive the acrid air quality. Did I make my point?

MEAT

<u>NEW HAMPSHIRE ROAST BEEF PIE</u> – Preheat oven to 450°F

★ **ADVANCED**

INGREDIENTS:

3 cups or about 1/3 pound roast beef from the deli – *diced*

3 T. bacon fat – or butter

1 large onion – *chopped*

¼ lb. fresh mushrooms – *sliced*

4 T. flour

2 cups beef broth (use the beef bouillon paste)

½ cup red wine

1 T. fresh parsley – *minced*

½ tsp. marjoram

1 tsp. Worcestershire sauce

<u>Salt & pepper</u>

Pastry crust – if using pre-made frozen, thaw while you make filling

DIRECTIONS:

1. Melt fat in **large skillet**. Sauté onions & mushrooms till tender
2. Stir in meat and sauté for one minute.
3. Sprinkle flour over all and blend well, stirring for one minute.
4. Pour in broth and wine. Stir till smooth. Filling should be thick like pot pie filling. If not thick enough, cook longer. If it's still not thick, mix flour with cold water, then add to mixture while stirring.
5. Season to taste; add Worcestershire sauce.
6. Pour into either a GREASED **2-quart casserole or a 10" pie plate**.
7. Top with pastry crust, and slash in 5 places to let out steam.
8. Bake at 450°f for 20 minutes or until crust looks done.

WHAT WE LEARNED:

✓ How to thicken filling. When you sprinkle flour over a mixture, you are mixing it well into the dish. Once liquid is added, though, you can't just add dry flour as it will get lumpy. That's why you mix flour (or cornstarch) well with cold water, THEN add to the mixture.

★

<u>**ORANGE BEEF**</u> – a stir fry recipe

★ **ADVANCED**

There is a lot of measuring and stove action, but the total time spent on this is only about 20 minutes. Save time by serving with 90-second rice.

SAUCE INGREDIENTS:

1 T. peanut oil

1 tsp. ginger – ground or the paste

1 jalapeno pepper – *minced* (or use canned chilies)

2 T. <u>concentrated</u> orange juice

¼ cup light brown sugar

¼ cup rice vinegar

¼ cup soy sauce

BEEF INGREDIENTS:

1 large egg white

1 T. cornstarch

1 pinch kosher salt – or to taste

1 lb. boneless rib-eye steak - *diced*

¼ cup peanut oil

6 scallions – *diced – separated into green parts & white parts*

DIRECTIONS:

1. Measure everything first, then start cooking.
2. In **large saucepan**, heat oil, add ginger & jalapeno & sauté 2-3 minutes.
3. Add OJ, sugar, vinegar, soy sauce; bring to a boil, then lower heat and simmer, stirring occasionally, until reduced by half (called reduction), about 10 minutes.
4. Combine egg white, cornstarch and salt in a **medium-sized bowl**. Add diced meat, tossing to coat meat with the batter.
5. In a **large skillet** over HIGH heat, heat oil till it shimmers, about 60 seconds, then add meat in a single layer and cook about 60-90 seconds.
6. Add white scallion pieces to pan; turn meat to other side. Cook 3 minutes. Pour orange sauce over meat and serve with rice. Top with green scallions.

WHAT WE LEARNED:

✓ That a reduction sauce is thickened into a concentrated sauce by cooking. It gets more intense through evaporation.

SALISBURY STEAK – Preheat oven to 350°F

★ MODERATELY EASY

No easy cookbook is complete without a cream of mushroom soup recipe. It's very church lady, but the late chef Tony Bourdain said he loved recipes like this. He thought they were homey and because he traveled so much, he appreciated it.

INGREDIENTS:

1-2/3 cup of saltines – *crushed*

2 lbs. ground beef

½ cup catsup

2 eggs – *beaten*

2 tsp. onion – *chopped fine*

2 tsp. fresh parsley – *chopped*

1 tsp. Worcestershire sauce

1-1/2 tsp. salt

½ tsp. each of marjoram, pepper, and nutmeg

SAUCE:

Garlic powder – dash

1 can cream of mushroom soup

1 cup milk

2 T. butter

1 tsp. sherry

4 oz. can sliced mushrooms – *drained*

1 T. chopped pimiento

DIRECTIONS:

1. In a **large bowl**, combine first 11 ingredients; mix well.
2. Shape into oval patties; place in BUTTERED **large, deep casserole dish**.
3. In **medium-sized saucepan**, heat soup with milk, butter, sherry, & garlic powder. Pour over patties. Cover with foil if your dish doesn't have a cover.
4. Bake COVERED at 350°F for 35 minutes. Add mushrooms and pimiento. Bake another 10 minutes.

MEAT LOAF TERIYAKI – microwave OR regular oven preheated to 350°F

★ **EASY**

INGREDIENTS:

2 lbs. lean ground beef

2 eggs – *lightly beaten*

2 slices bread – *soaked in water and squeezed dry*

½ cup green pepper – *chopped*

1 medium onion – *finely chopped* OR 1T. onion powder

Garlic powder

2 T. soy sauce

2 T. brown sugar

2 T. lemon juice – *fresh squeezed*

1 T. fresh parsley – *chopped*

¾ tsp. ground ginger – or ginger paste

TOPPING:

1 T. brown sugar & 1 T. soy sauce, mixed together

MICROWAVE DIRECTIONS:

1. In a **large mixing bowl**, combine all ingredients except topping and blend well. Wear disposable gloves and blend with hands.
2. Spoon into a **6-cup ring mold OR** arrange in a circle in an UNGREASED **large casserole**.
3. Cook on HIGH 15 minutes. Meat loaf is done when it begins to pull away slightly from sides of dish.
4. Let stand 5 minutes. Pour off juices. Invert onto heated serving platter.
5. Spoon topping over top and garnish with parsley.

REGULAR OVEN DIRECTIONS:

Bake in an UNGREASED **loaf pan** at 350°F for 45 minutes. Take out of oven and put on topping. Bake another 10 minutes or until thermometer says 165°F.

WHAT WE LEARNED:

✓ Letting the cooked meat stand for a few minutes allows the juices to settle and redistribute throughout the meat. It will retain its juiciness.

✓ You don't need to grease the pans because the meat creates plenty of grease.

★

JEANNE'S MEAT LOAF – preheat oven to 350°F

★ **EASY**

This recipe comes from my husband's college classmate. His late wife used to make this. It is simple and delicious. The leftovers will make a nice sandwich the next day.

INGREDIENTS:

1 egg

½ cup milk

1/3 cup dry bread crumbs

2 T. onion – *finely chopped*

½ tsp. salt

1/8 tsp. pepper

¼ tsp. ground mustard

¼ tsp. garlic salt

1 tsp. Worcestershire sauce

1 lb. ground beef

OPTIONAL: 2 strips bacon

DIRECTIONS:

1. In a large mixing bowl, beat egg, then add the rest of the ingredients, mixing well.
2. Add the meat last. Mix well, using your hands to incorporate all ingredients.
3. Place into an UNGREASED meat loaf pan. (I like a loaf pan with drop down sides)
4. Bake 40 minutes. If using uncooked bacon, place on top of meat loaf at the *beginning* of cooking. If using pre-cooked bacon, place bacon strips on top *after* cooking for 40 minutes.
5. Bake till temperature reaches 160°F. Drain grease before serving. Serves 2-3.

WHAT WE LEARNED:

✓ Mixing the meat in last ensures that the wet ingredients and spices are thoroughly mixed together.

MEATLOAF MINIS – Preheat oven to 350°F

★ **EASY**

INGREDIENTS:

½ cup onion – *grated*

7 T. ketchup – *divided*

1-1/4 lbs. ground hamburg or meat loaf mix

2 eggs – *beaten*

½ cup **quick** cooking oats

2 tsp. garlic powder

1 tsp. salt

DIRECTIONS:

1. Line 9 compartments of a **muffin tin** with baking cups OR spray with nonstick spray.
2. Combine all ingredients EXCEPT 3 T. of ketchup in a mixing bowl. Distribute mixture evenly among cups.
3. Using a **pastry brush,** put 1 tsp. ketchup on each mini-meatloaf.
4. Bake until firm with lightly browned edges, 30-35 minutes.

WHAT WE LEARNED:

✓ Meat loaf mix is a combination of ground hamburg, ground pork, and veal or turkey. For some reason, this mixture of different kinds of meat makes an extra delicious meatloaf or meatball.

✓ Cooking in individual servings in a muffin tin makes it easy to serve.

APPLESAUCE MEATBALLS – Preheat oven to 350°F

★ **EASY**

INGREDIENTS:

1 lb. ground hamburg

1/3 cup onion – *chopped fine*

1 egg – *beaten*

½ cup corn flakes

¼ cup apple sauce (plain)

Salt & pepper

1 medium can tomato sauce

DIRECTIONS:

1. In **medium-sized mixing bowl**, blend all ingredients except tomato sauce.
2. Form into meatballs.
3. Place into a GREASED **casserole dish**.
4. Pour tomato sauce over all.
5. Bake at 350°F for 45 minutes.

WHAT WE LEARNED:

✓ That applesauce enhances the meat deliciously.

✓ Wear disposable gloves when forming meatballs if you wish.

✓ Try using an ice cream scoop to make the meatballs. If they are of uniform size, they will all cook evenly.

★

SPICED LAMB MEATBALLS – Broiler and crockpot

★ **EASY**

INGREDIENTS:

1-1/2 lbs. ground lamb, not too lean OR meatball mix

½ cup breadcrumbs

2 tsp. kosher salt

½ tsp. ground black pepper

½ cup red onion – *finely diced*

1 tsp. ground cumin

1 tsp. ground coriander

¼ tsp. cinnamon or allspice

½ tsp. nutmeg

1 cup chicken broth

Dried mint and dill for garnish

Plain yogurt for garnish

DIRECTIONS:

1. In a **large bowl**, use your hands to combine meat, breadcrumbs, salt, pepper, onion, cumin, coriander, and cinnamon.
2. Form into meatballs (walnut sized). Makes about 30. Put on UNGREASED **cookie sheet**.
3. **Broil in oven** till light brown—5 to 10 minutes. Broiling seals in the juices and gives the meat a headstart.
4. Put meatballs into **crockpot** with 1 cup of chicken broth.
5. Cook on LOW in crockpot for 4 hours, basting occasionally with broth.
6. Serve with plain yogurt, sprinkled with mint and dill, for garnish.

WHAT WE LEARNED:

✓ This tastes more Greek if made with lamb, but if you use other meats, the spices will still make it taste Greek.

✓ Serve with rice pilaf and a Greek Salad.

★

PORK BALLS CANTONESE – Preheat oven to 350°F

★ **ADVANCED**

MEATBALL INGREDIENTS:

1-1/2 lbs. ground pork

2/3 cup evaporated milk

¼ cup onion - *finely chopped*

1 tsp. salt

Dash of pepper

MEATBALL DIRECTIONS:

1. In a **large mixing bowl,** mix all ingredients together. Shape into 12 meatballs.
2. Place in an UNGREASED **roasting pan** (they will make their own grease). Bake 35-40 minutes or until nicely browned.
3. While meatballs are cooking, make the Sweet-Sour Sauce.

Pork Balls Cantonese continued . . .

SWEET-SOUR SAUCE INGREDIENTS:

1 can (13-14 oz.) pineapple – *crushed*

¼ cup vinegar

¼ cup sugar

2 tsp. soy sauce

2 T. water – cold }

1-1/2 Tablespoons cornstarch }

1 T. butter

1 cup celery – *sliced*

½ cup scallions – *chopped (cut with scissors)*

½ cup green pepper strips – *cut ¼ inch wide*

1 large tomato – *cut in wedges*

SWEET-SOUR SAUCE DIRECTIONS:

1. Into a **2-qt. saucepan**, drain juice from pineapple. Save pineapple.
2. Add vinegar, sugar, and soy sauce to pan.
3. In a **small bowl** blend cold water and cornstarch. Add to pineapple juice mixture.
4. Cook over MEDIUM heat, stirring constantly with a wire **whisk**, until mixture is thick and clear.
5. Cook 2 additional minutes. Stir in butter.
6. About 10 minutes before serving, carefully stir in drained pineapple, celery, onions, green pepper and tomato.
7. Continue cooking over VERY LOW HEAT just until vegetables are heated.
8. Serve meatballs over rice, then pour sweet-sour sauce on top. Garnish with chopped almonds if desired.

WHAT WE LEARNED:

✓ How to coordinate a two-part recipe.

✓ How to thicken a sauce using cold water and cornstarch, seeing it turn from a pile of ingredients into a beautiful, clear sauce.

SCANDINAVIAN MEATBALLS – Crockpot

★ **EASY**

INGREDIENTS:

1 lb. ground hamburg

1/3 cup onion – *chopped*

1 egg – *beaten*

¼ cup **quick** oatmeal

1/3 cup milk

1 T. parsley

¼ tsp. salt

1/8 tsp. pepper

1/8 tsp. allspice

1/8 tsp. nutmeg

DIRECTIONS:

1. In **large mixing bowl** mix all ingredients together. Make meatballs. Place in crockpot.
2. Pour ¼ cup beef broth over all. There should be some liquid in the bottom of the crockpot. Add more liquid if necessary.
3. Cook in crockpot for 1-2 hours on LOW OR ½ to 1 hour on HIGH.
4. If cooking in a regular oven, cook at 425°F for 15 minutes. Meat thermometer should read 165°F, whichever cooking method is used.
5. Serve with egg noodles and top with sour cream as a garnish. A green vegetable goes nicely with this dish.

SWEDISH MEATBALLS – stovetop recipe

★ **ADVANCED**

INGREDIENTS:

1 cup fine bread crumbs – *crunch up your own with stale bread*

2-1/2 cups milk

2 lbs. ground beef

1 cup onion – *finely chopped*

2 eggs – *slightly beaten*

1-1/2 tsp. salt

¼ tsp. pepper

1 tsp. nutmeg

1 stick butter

¼ cup flour

3 tsp. beef bouillon paste }

3 c. hot water }

1-1/2 cups light cream (or milk)

DIRECTIONS:

1. In **large mixing bowl** soften bread crumbs in 1 cup milk. Add beef, onion, eggs, and seasonings. Mix thoroughly.
2. Shape into 1-inch meatballs, using small ice cream scoop.
3. Heat butter in **large skillet**; add meatballs a few at a time. Don't crowd the pan. Brown on all sides. Remove meatballs and keep warm.
4. **Whisk** flour into drippings in pan. Blend well. Cook 60 seconds.
5. In **4-cup glass measuring cup** dissolve bouillon paste into hot water. Gradually add to flour mixture in pan, stirring constantly with **whisk** until smooth. DON'T WALK AWAY.
6. Add remaining milk and cream to pan. Cook over LOW HEAT, stirring constantly for 3 minutes. Add meatballs. Simmer on LOW HEAT for 10-15 minutes, stirring occasionally. Serve with egg noodles, rice or mashed potatoes.

WHAT WE LEARNED:

✓ How to make gravy.

SOMBRERO DIP OR ENTRÉE – a Microwave recipe

★ MODERATELY EASY

This is great for a party dip. If you want to puree the entire recipe, that makes it easy to eat. If serving for supper, have it with rice, tortilla chips, shredded lettuce and diced tomato.

INGREDIENTS:

1 lb. lean ground beef

1 large onion – *chopped*

½ cup catsup

1 T. chili powder

1 tsp. garlic salt or powder

1 tsp. ground cumin

1 tsp. dried oregano

One 24 oz. can kidney beans – *UNDRAINED and pureed*

One 2 oz. jar pimiento-stuffed green olives – *sliced & divided*

½ lb. cheddar cheese – *grated* (for garnish)

4 scallions – *chopped* (for garnish)

DIRECTIONS:

1. Combine beef and onion in UNGREASED **2-quart casserole** and cook in microwave on HIGH 5 minutes, stirring once to crumble beef.
2. Add catsup, chili powder, garlic, cumin, oregano, and blend well.
3. Puree beans in **food processor or blender** and stir into beef mixture.
4. Cover and cook on HIGH 10 minutes, stirring once halfway through.
5. Blend in about ¾ of the olive slices.
6. Garnish with cheese and remaining olives. Serve hot.

SHOULDER LAMB CHOPS WITH MANDARIN ORANGES

– Preheat oven to 350°F

★ **RIDICULOUSLY EASY** – Just add a vegetable or salad and call it a meal.

INGREDIENTS:

4 thick shoulder lamb chops

1 cup rice – UNCOOKED (NOT brown rice)

2 tangerines – peeled, separated in segments OR 1 can of Mandarin oranges

2-1/2 cups beef bouillon – use beef paste

½ tsp. dried mint

Salt and pepper

———————————

DIRECTIONS:

1. BUTTER a **low-sided casserole dish or 13" x 9" pan**.
2. Heat a **large frying pan** for 60 seconds. Put lamb chops in pan and sear briefly in their own fat, just a minute or two on each side. Lamb is a fatty meat, so you do not need butter or oil to fry.
3. Place UNCOOKED white rice in the bottom of the buttered casserole.
4. Place chops over rice and arrange oranges on top.
5. Pour in bouillon and sprinkle mint, salt and pepper on top.
6. Cover and bake at 350°F for 45 minutes. Serves 4.

WHAT WE LEARNED:

✓ How the lamb was seared is called braising. It browns the outside of the chop and seals in the juices. They will cook through in the rest of the recipe.

✓ The rice will cook in the broth in the oven and will be flavored with the meat juices for an almost one-pot meal.

★

HAM IN MUSTARD SAUCE – stovetop

★ EASY

INGREDIENTS:

1 lb. ham (about 3 cups) – *fully cooked and diced*

1/3 cup butter (5-1/3 T. of a stick)

1/3 cup flour

3 cups milk

1-3/4 cups (10 oz. pkg) frozen peas – *cooked & drained*

2 T. mustard

Toast – *quartered* (aka "toast points")

DIRECTIONS:

1. Dice ham.
2. Cook peas.
3. Melt butter in **large saucepan. Whisk** in flour. Cook for 60 seconds.
4. Whisk milk gradually into the flour/butter mixture.
5. Cook over MEDIUM heat, stirring constantly with a whisk until mixture just comes to a boil and thickens.
6. Stir in ham, peas, and mustard.
7. Serve over toast points. Garnish with paprika.

WHAT WE LEARNED:

✓ How to make a roux and turn it into a nice sauce, which is the basis for this and many recipes.

POULTRY

MARY'S CHICKEN CROQUETTES

★ ADVANCED

This recipe is from my late mother-in-law. Make these in stages.

SAUCE INGREDIENTS:

4 T. butter (1/2 a stick)

5 T. flour

1 cup milk

½ cup chicken broth – *saved from cooking the chicken*

4 chicken thighs (should make 3 cups when diced)

1 to 2 tsp. onion – *minced*

Salt & pepper

1 T. parsley

½ tsp. ground thyme

1 egg

2 T. milk or cream

1 cup bread crumbs – plain or Italian

Oil for frying

DIRECTIONS:

1. Boil chicken till it tests 165°F with the meat thermometer. Save the broth. Cool chicken in refrigerator, then dice. (Don't overcook chicken or it will be tough.)
2. In **large saucepan**, make a sauce with the first 4 ingredients: melt butter, add flour. Cook 1 minute, then add milk and broth. Should be thick. Cool.
3. In **large mixing bowl**, mix diced chicken, onion and seasoning with sauce. Cool in fridge.
4. Form croquettes. Rectangular shape is traditional, but if you want flatter patties, that's OK, too. Put back in fridge to firm up (30-60 minutes)
5. Lay out **two shallow bowls**, like pasta bowls. Put egg and milk in one bowl and mix well. Put crumbs into the other bowl.
6. Dip croquette into egg mixture, then crumbs. Freeze them at this point if desired, preferably in one layer or with wax paper between layers.
7. In **large frying pan**, fry in oil until golden brown. DON'T WALK AWAY, but keep a close eye on them; turn once. They fry up in less than 10 minutes. If cooking from frozen, thaw a bit first before frying.

WHAT WE LEARNED:

✓ Keep fried croquettes warm in the oven at 200°F till everything is ready. Serve with chicken gravy or cream of chicken soup thinned with milk.

CHICKEN PARMESAN – Preheat oven to 350°F. Butter **large shallow casserole**.

★ MODERATELY EASY

Whether you make this with chicken, veal, or turkey cutlets, it turns out perfectly.

INGREDIENTS:

1-1/2 lbs. boneless, skinless chicken breasts

¼ cup flour

1 tsp. salt * 1/8 tsp. pepper

1 egg – *beaten*

2 T. milk

<u>1 cup dry bread crumbs</u>

1/3 cup olive oil

4 T. butter

½ cup onion – *chopped*

6 oz. can tomato paste

1-1/4 cup water

½ tsp. dried basil

½ tsp. dried oregano

<u>½ tsp. salt</u>

4 T. Parmesan – *grated*

Sliced cheese for topping – I like cheddar, some like Mozzarella. You do you.

DIRECTIONS:

1. Cut chicken into serving-size pieces. Pound thin.
2. Lay out **3 shallow bowls**. Into one, mix flour with salt & pepper.
3. Into 2nd bowl, put egg, beaten with the 2 T. of milk.
4. Into 3rd bowl put bread crumbs. Dip the meat into flour, then egg, then crumbs.
5. In **large skillet**, heat olive oil for 1 minute. Brown the meat on both sides till golden; don't overcook, as it is

going into the oven. Transfer to **casserole**.

6. Add butter to the same skillet. Brown onion about 5 minutes.
7. Add tomato paste, water, spices, ½ tsp. salt. Bring to a boil, then SIMMER 5 minutes. Taste it to see if it's seasoned enough.
8. Sprinkle cutlets with Parmesan cheese, spoon tomato sauce over meat.
9. Bake at 350°F 15 minutes. Take out and top with cheese. Bake 5 more minutes.

CHICKEN PICCATA - stovetop

★ MODERATELY EASY

Not something to be made in advance, but you can still measure the ingredients and get it ready to go. Fry at the last minute for fresh, lemony deliciousness.

INGREDIENTS:

4 boneless, skinless chicken breasts or thighs

2 T. Parmesan

1/3 cup flour

Salt & pepper

4 T. olive oil

4 T. butter

½ cup chicken stock OR white wine

3 T. lemon juice – about 1 lemon

¼ cup brined capers (comes in a jar) - UNDRAINED

DIRECTIONS:

1. Pound meat until it's thin.
2. In a **shallow bowl** mix flour, salt & pepper, and Parmesan.
3. Dredge meat in flour mixture.
4. In **large skillet**, heat olive oil and 2 T. butter for 1 minute over MEDIUM HEAT. Add chicken and brown well—about 3 minutes per side. DON'T WALK AWAY.
5. Remove chicken, reserve on a plate and keep it warm.
6. Add chicken stock/wine, lemon juice, capers to skillet. Use a **spatula** to scrape the browned bits (deglazing). Reduce sauce by half.* **Whisk** in remaining 2 T. butter.
7. Serve with sauce poured over the chicken OR on the side in little dipping bowls.

WHAT WE LEARNED:

*Simply cooking a sauce for 5-10 minutes will reduce it, thickening it, hence the term "reduction sauce."

CHICKEN CACCIATORE - stovetop

★ MODERATELY EASY

Using peanut oil instead of other oils makes a big difference in the taste.

INGREDIENTS

6 chicken thighs – with skin

Flour

¼ cup peanut oil

1 cup sliced onion

½ cup green pepper – *sliced*

15 oz. can tomato sauce

¾ cup water

1 T. parsley

½ tsp. dried oregano

½ tsp. thyme

¾ tsp. salt

Black pepper to taste

¼ lb. mushrooms – *sliced*

DIRECTIONS:

1. Put flour in a **resealable bag**, then chicken. Close bag. Shake till chicken is coated.
2. In **large skillet**, heat peanut oil – about 2 minutes.
3. Brown chicken on both sides, then remove from pan to a **platter**.
4. In the same pan and drippings, sauté onion and green pepper till tender.
5. Add tomato sauce, water and spices.
6. Add chicken back to frying pan; COVER skillet and cook on LOW HEAT for 45 minutes, stirring occasionally.
7. Add mushrooms and cook UNCOVERED another 15 minutes.

CHICKEN TARRAGON - Stovetop

★ EASY

INGREDIENTS:

2 boneless chicken breasts – *pounded thin*

½ cup flour

4 tsp. butter

1 T. dried tarragon

Salt & pepper

1 cup white wine

DIRECTIONS:

1. Pound chicken breasts till thin. Pat dry.
2. Put flour in a **shallow bowl**. Dredge chicken parts through flour.
3. In **large skillet**, melt butter. Brown chicken on both sides. Takes only about 3 minutes per side.
4. In **measuring cup**, mix wine, tarragon, salt & pepper and pour over chicken in the skillet.
5. Simmer UNCOVERED about 15 minutes.
6. Remove chicken from drippings; put on **platter** and keep warm.
7. Simmer drippings for a minute to reduce, then **whisk** in ¼ cup heavy cream and stir well till heated through, about 1 minute. Serve sauce in individual bowls for dipping.

WHAT WE LEARNED:

✓ That chicken, pounded thin, cooks fast.

✓ That a little cream thickens a sauce.

✓ That just one herb can flavor the whole dish.

★

HONEY-LEMON CHICKEN – Preheat oven to 425°F. Broiler pan with insert.

★ **EASY**

INGREDIENTS:

2 lbs. chicken quarters or thighs

½ cup honey

¼ cup butter – *melted*

2 T. lemon juice – about half a lemon

1-1/2 tsp. dried parsley

¼ tsp. thyme

¼ tsp. rosemary

———————————

DIRECTIONS:

1. In a **pourable mixing bowl or measuring cup**, mix all ingredients together except chicken.
2. Place chicken on a plate in a **resealable food storage bag**.
3. Cover chicken with 2/3 of the honey mixture; close up bag tight. Marinade for 2-4 hours in refrigerator. Turn over once.
4. On **broiler pan**, place chicken SKIN SIDE UP on broiler insert.
5. BAKE first side till golden brown at 425°F 15-17 minutes.
6. Turn chicken over and continue to bake the second side 14-16 minutes.
7. Brush the remaining honey mixture on chicken the last 2-4 minutes of baking.

NOTE: The oven will get very hot as the chicken juices will smoke a bit. Use your oven's exhaust fan at beginning of cooking.

WHAT WE LEARNED:

✓ That marinating makes meat juicy.

★

COUNTRY STYLE CHICKEN KIEV – Preheat oven to 375°F.

★ **MODERATELY EASY**

INGREDIENTS:

½ cup fine dry bread crumbs

2 T. grated Parmesan

1 tsp. dried basil

1 tsp. dried oregano

½ tsp. garlic powder

¼ tsp. salt

2/3 cup butter (about 1 stick + 2 T.) - *melted*

2 chicken breasts (about 1-1/2 lbs.)

¼ cup white wine OR apple juice

¼ cup scallions – *cut with scissors*

¼ cup fresh parsley – *chopped*

DIRECTIONS:

1. In a **shallow bowl**, combine bread crumbs, Parmesan, basil, oregano, garlic powder, and salt.
2. In **another shallow bowl**, put melted butter.
3. Dip chicken in melted butter, then crumb mixture. Reserve remaining butter.
4. Place chicken skin side up in UNGREASED **9" square baking pan**.
5. Bake 50-60 minutes till chicken is fork tender.
6. While chicken is baking, add wine, scallions, and parsley to melted butter.
7. When chicken is cooked, pour butter sauce over chicken and bake another 3 to 5 minutes or until sauce is heated through. YIELD: 4 servings.

NOTE: Since raw chicken touched the butter, <u>never</u> taste the butter or the later mixture. Putting it in the oven for 3-5 minutes at the end will cook it properly.

Anything that touches raw chicken should always be cleaned and sanitized, including the sink and countertops.

★

CHIEF ENGINEER McANDREW'S OVEN FRIED CHICKEN – Preheat to 350°F

★ MODERATELY EASY

This is a recipe from one of my husband's Mass. Maritime colleagues. As Chief Engineer on many types of oceangoing vessels, he was sometimes called upon to do the cooking on a ship with a small crew. He developed this after years of tweaking and, since there was never a mutiny while he sailed, it can be considered a huge success! It is easy, buttery, and delicious. It goes in and out of the oven a few times.

INGREDIENTS:

6 chicken drumsticks or thighs

1 cup flour

1 cup seasoned bread crumbs

1 stick unsalted butter

1 tsp. poultry seasoning – or make your own with salt, pepper, onion powder, garlic powder, thyme and oregano

DIRECTIONS:

1. Put flour in shallow bowl. Dip chicken and coat thoroughly.
2. Place in roasting pan (not glass or ceramic!) and bake at 350°F for 15 minutes.
3. Melt the butter—either in microwave or top of stove.
4. Take chicken out of oven and pour half the butter over it, covering whatever flour is showing.
5. Now sprinkle seasonings on top of chicken.
6. Put back in oven and cook for another 15 minutes.
7. Take out the chicken and pour remaining butter over it for another coat.
8. Sprinkle the breadcrumbs on top of the buttered chicken.
9. Bake the final 20 minutes till temperature reaches 175°F
10. Put under the broiler for about 2 minutes or till skin crisps a little.

NOTES:

✓ This is a great dish for a big gathering. You can make a big pan of chicken and cook all at once. Serve in the same pan to keep it hot and allow guests to scoop up some of the melted butter.

✓ Never put a ceramic or glass dish under the broiler or it will break.

<u>CHICKEN SHORTCAKE</u> - stovetop

★ MODERATELY EASY

This comfort-food recipe is from the Shakers, a religious sect that has almost died out. The dish has a 19th century look to it, perfect for a cold winter's evening.

INGREDIENTS:

1 large chicken, boiled in water to cover

2 cups chicken stock

2 T. flour / 3 T. water – *mixed to make a paste*

1 lb. mushrooms – *sliced*

2 T. butter – *melted*

¼ tsp. salt

Black pepper to taste

1 recipe for corn bread – *baked*

DIRECTIONS:

1. Remove the skin and bones from cooked chicken and dice or shred meat. If you don't want to do this part, just buy a roast chicken from the supermarket and use pre-made chicken stock.
2. In a **large saucepan**, make a sauce using 2 cups of chicken stock, brought to a boil. Then put in the flour/ water paste. Cook at least one minute or until thick.
3. In a **medium frying pan**, sauté mushrooms in butter.
4. Add diced chicken and mushrooms to the sauce. Season with salt & pepper, thyme, rosemary, sage as desired.
5. Cut corn bread into 4 inch squares, split and butter. Cover with chicken mixture. YIELD: 6 servings.

GINGER LIME CHICKEN - stovetop

★ **EASY**

INGREDIENTS:

1-1/2 to 2 lbs. boneless, skinless chicken thighs or breasts – or Pork cutlets!

Salt & black pepper

1/3 cup mayonnaise

1 T. lime zest – from 2 limes, plus lime wedges for serving*

1 T. finely grated fresh ginger OR 1 tsp. ginger paste**

DIRECTIONS:

1. Pat meat dry and season all over with salt.
2. In a **medium bowl**, stir together the mayo, lime zest and ginger. Season with salt & pepper.
3. Add meat to the mayo mixture and stir to coat. Marinate up to 8 hours in fridge if you like.
4. Heat a **large skillet** over MEDIUM HIGH HEAT. Cook meat until juices run clear, about 5 minutes per side or till it is at least 165°F as tested with meat thermometer.

WHAT WE LEARNED:

✓ Cut the presentation lime wedges first and save to put on the plate, then zest the other ones. Use a special tool to get the skin off a lime (or lemon) in little bits. If you don't have one, use a vegetable peeler.

✓ Ginger paste can be found in the produce section. It's very handy.

FISH

EASY SCAMPI - stovetop

★ EASY

INGREDIENTS:

¾ cup (1-1/2 sticks) unsalted butter

¼ cup onion – *finely chopped*

3 to 4 garlic cloves – *crushed* or ½ tsp. garlic powder

4 sprigs fresh parsley – *chopped*

1 lb. medium shrimp – raw, deveined (you can buy like this)

¼ cup dry white wine

2 T. fresh lemon juice (about half a lemon)

Salt and pepper

DIRECTIONS:

1. In **medium sized skillet**, melt butter over LOW HEAT.
2. Add onion, garlic, and parsley and sauté until golden, about 10 minutes.
3. Add shrimp and stir, cooking just until it turns pink.
4. Remove shrimp and place in **ovenproof dish**. Cover lightly and keep warm.
5. Add wine and lemon juice to skillet and simmer about 2-3 minutes. Season to taste with salt & pepper and pour over shrimp. YIELD: 4 servings.

WHAT WE LEARNED:

✓ How quickly you can make this elegant dish. The whole thing probably takes about 15 minutes. Set the table first and get your side dishes ready before even cooking this!

CRAB & CHEDDAR CASSEROLE – Preheat oven to 350°F

★ EASY

SAUCE INGREDIENTS:

3 T. flour

1 cup skim milk

¼ tsp. dry mustard

1/8 tsp. each of salt & pepper

3 oz. cheddar cheese

2 T. dry sherry (or any sweet wine)

2 small cans crabmeat – splurge for the good stuff – *drained*

3 T. of jalapeno peppers/mild chilies – *chopped fine*

2 T. butter – *melted }Topping: Just mix together*

15 crackers (I like Ritz) – *crushed }*

DIRECTIONS:

1. Spray a **1-quart casserole** with non-stick spray.
2. In a **small saucepan**, **whisk** together all ingredients for sauce and cook over MEDIUM HEAT, stirring constantly till mixture thickens. Remove from heat.
3. Add cheese and stir till cheese is melted. Add crabmeat and peppers.
4. Pour into casserole dish and top with buttered cracker crumbs.
5. Bake uncovered for 20 minutes.

NOTE: Some people rinse canned crabmeat first, to lessen the salt content. A review of various FDA guidelines did not produce this suggestion or requirement. So rinse if you like. The crabmeat is fully cooked, so you only need to drain it for any recipe.

★

REAL CAJUN CRABMEAT AU GRATIN – Preheat oven to 350°F

★ **EASY**

Using cream-of-anything soup in a recipe smacks of church lady recipes from the 1950s, which is a fair characterization. However, the late Culinary Institute of America-trained chef Tony Bourdain said he loved these types of homey recipes.* And the Cajuns are all about things tasting good, so make it and enjoy it!

INGREDIENTS:

1 cup sliced mushrooms – fresh or canned

¼ cup onions – *chopped*

2 T. butter

One 10-1/2 oz. can of condensed cream of celery soup

1 T. sherry

1 can (6 oz. +) crabmeat – *drained*

¼ cup cheese – *shredded*

DIRECTIONS:

1. In **medium skillet** over MEDIUM HEAT sauté onions and mushrooms in butter until tender.
2. Stir in soup, sherry, and crabmeat. Cook while stirring for 5 minutes.
3. Pour mixture into GREASED **baking dish or au gratin pan.**
4. Bake at 350°F for 10-15 minutes. Remove from oven.
5. Sprinkle with cheese. Bake 5 more minutes or until cheese is melted.

WHAT WE LEARNED:

*How not to be a food snob. In that same vein, I was assistant to a baker in a major franchisor and I baked him a birthday cake from a mix. I apologized to him for making it from a mix, but he said "It tasted good and everyone loved it, so don't apologize for it. Plus it was thoughtful of you to make it."

SAUTEED SCALLOPS – Stovetop. Serves 4. Preheat oven to 250°F

★ EASY

Don't be fooled by the long list of spices. Once you measure them out, this recipe cooks up quickly. Set the table and get your side dishes ready. Cook this last.

INGREDIENTS:

{ 2 T. flour

Put all in resealable bag: { ½ tsp. salt

{ ½ tsp. onion powder

{ ¼ tsp. white pepper

{ ¼ tsp. garlic powder

{ ¼ tsp. ground thyme

{ Pinch of paprika, marjoram, sage, cayenne pepper

1 lb. sea scallops (the big ones)

3 T. unsalted butter

1 T. oil

6 oz. (3/4 cup) white wine

2 T. lemon juice (about half a lemon)

1 T. unsalted butter

Salt

3 T. fresh parsley – *chopped*

DIRECTIONS:

1. Using a **colander**, rinse scallops with cold water. Drain and pat dry.
2. In **large skillet,** heat butter and oil over MEDIUM HEAT.
3. Shake fish in plastic bag with spices. Place in skillet and sauté on HIGH HEAT for only 3-4 minutes. Test one for doneness—cut in half. It should be opaque.
4. Remove scallops with **slotted spoon** to a **platter**. Keep warm in oven.
5. Cook pan drippings over HIGH heat till golden, 1 minute.
6. Add wine and cook, **whisking** constantly to deglaze the pan.
7. Reduce to LOW. Simmer UNCOVERED till slightly thick, about 3 minutes.
8. Whisk in lemon juice, butter, salt & pepper. Pour sauce over scallops.

WHAT WE LEARNED:

✓ Buy the best scallops you can at a fish market or reputable grocer. They should smell pleasant. Use within 3 days. Don't overcook. They are expensive, so you don't want to have to throw them out.

DEBBIE O'S COQUILLES ST. JACQUES MORNAY – Stovetop & broiler

★ ADVANCED

There are a lot of steps in this recipe and it requires your full attention. That being the case, set the table first and make your side dishes easy—like baked potatoes, pre-made salad, or vegetables you can just pop in the microwave.

INGREDIENTS:

1 cup dry white wine

½ tsp. salt

<u>1 lb. sea scallops (the big ones)</u>

2 T. onion – *chopped*

¼ lb. mushrooms – *sliced*

<u>¼ cup butter (½ stick)</u>

¼ cup flour

½ cup heavy cream

<u>2 T. lemon juice (about half a lemon)</u>

1/3 cup Swiss cheese

1-2 T. fresh parsley – chopped

{ ½ cup bread crumbs or cracker crumbs

Make buttered crumbs: { 1 T. butter – melted

DIRECTIONS:

1. In **small saucepan**, bring wine to boiling. Add salt and scallops; COVER.
2. Simmer scallops just till tender—5 to 6 minutes. Don't overcook! Drain, saving 1 cup of the liquid.
3. In **medium-sized saucepan**, sauté onion and mushrooms in butter till soft, then remove from heat; stir in flour till smooth. Gradually **whisk** in reserved scallop liquid. Put back on the burner and cook, stirring constantly till sauce thickens and bubbles—just 1 minute.
4. Stir in cream and lemon juice. Bring to a boil; immediately remove from heat.
5. Add scallops, Swiss cheese and parsley to sauce; spoon into BUTTERED **suitable-for-broiling casserole**. Top with buttered bread crumbs and broil 4 to 6 inches from broiler, just till slightly golden. DON'T WALK AWAY, as it broils fast.

WHAT WE LEARNED:

✓ Organizational skills in a multi-part recipe.

✓ The benefit of super easy side dishes when making a recipe like this.

MAPLE SALMON

★ **RIDICULOUSLY EASY**

Even if you're not a big fan of salmon, this is ridiculously easy and very delicious. I prefer the salmon **filets**, as they have far fewer bones.

INGREDIENTS:

¼ cup maple syrup

2 T. soy sauce

½ tsp. garlic powder

1 tsp. onion powder

¼ tsp. salt

1/8 tsp. black pepper

1 tsp. dried dill

1 lb. salmon

DIRECTIONS:

1. In a **small bowl**, mix the maple syrup, soy sauce, garlic, and salt & pepper.
2. Place salmon in a **shallow glass baking dish** and coat with the maple mixture.
3. Cover the dish and marinate in the refrigerator for 30 minutes, turning once (after 15 minutes).
4. Preheat oven to 400°F while salmon is marinating.
5. Place baking dish in oven and bake UNCOVERED for 20 minutes or until easily flaked with fork.

NOTE:

20 minutes cooking time is for a convection oven, which cooks a bit faster than a conventional oven. If you don't have a convection oven (fan in the back for even circulation) cook an extra 5 minutes at a time until it's done.

★

LINDA'S SALMON PATTIES – Stovetop

★ EASY

I don't know who Linda is but she makes a mean pattie! You could even put these in a sandwich.

INGREDIENTS:

One 3.75 oz. can of Red Fancy Blueback Salmon – *rinsed and drained*

1 cooked potato (skin on is OK) – *mashed*

1 egg – *beaten*

1/3 cup herb seasoned stuffing

2 T. fresh parsley – *chopped*

2 T. onion – *minced fine*

1/8 tsp. garlic powder

¼ tsp. salt

DIRECTIONS:

1. In **medium-sized mixing bowl**, mix all ingredients together.
2. Make patties either with your hands or a **hamburger mold**. It will make 4.
3. Heat **large frying pan** for 60 seconds. Add 2 T. peanut oil. Heat another 60 seconds.
4. Put patties in pan and fry about 3 minutes per side.

WHAT WE LEARNED:

✓ They say we should eat more salmon. This is a good way to do this.

SCALLOPS PICCATA – stovetop

★ EASY

INGREDIENTS:

12 fresh sea scallops – serves 2

Sea salt

Black pepper

¼ cup olive oil

3 T. unsalted butter

1 T. mild onion or scallions – *chopped fine*

2 T. capers – *rinsed and drained*

2 T. lemon juice – (about half a lemon)

1/3 cup flat leaf parsley leaves – *finely chopped*

DIRECTIONS:

1. Rinse scallops and pat dry with paper towel. Season with salt and pepper.
2. Heat a **large sauté pan** over MEDIUM-HIGH HEAT for 60 seconds, then add oil. After 30 seconds, add scallops. Don't crowd the pan but work in batches if necessary.
3. Sauté scallops until well browned, only about 2 minutes per side. Test one for doneness—cut in half. It should be opaque.
4. When done, transfer to a **platter**, cover and keep warm.
5. Return large sauté pan to heat, add the 3 T. of butter and cook for 30 seconds. Add scallions and capers, sauté for 1 minute.
6. Add lemon juice carefully (to avoid splattering) and chopped parsley.
7. Pour sauce over scallops or put in little individual bowls for dipping.

WHAT WE LEARNED:

✓ That scallops piccata is as good as chicken piccata if you like savory things.

✓ That you should cook this at the last minute while guests are finishing their appetizers, because it cooks that fast.

★

FRIED FISH

★ MODERATELY EASY

In the mood for fish & chips? No need to pay high restaurant prices. This goes up pretty quick if you can get someone else to make the fries (see Ricky's French Fries in the Starch chapter). It's actually easy, but **if you're new to cooking, you need to exert caution and attention to frying in hot oil.**

INGREDIENTS:

1 lb. white fish (serves about 2) such as Tilapia, Haddock, Cod

Flour for dredging

Salt & pepper

Dried dill

Onion powder – to taste

Canola oil for frying

1. DIRECTIONS: Rinse fish, pat dry.
2. In a **shallow bowl**, put the flour and spices.
3. Dredge the fish pieces through the flour till coated on both sides.
4. Heat a **heavy bottomed large frying pan** for 60 seconds. Put in oil and heat another 60 seconds.
5. Now put each piece in, placing away from you to avoid getting splattered.
6. Cook, turning once with **tongs**, till both sides are golden brown, up to 6 minutes per side. DON'T WALK AWAY, but monitor its progress closely.

WHAT WE LEARNED:

✓ Use an oil with a high smoking point such as canola, corn, safflower, peanut, avocado, or grapeseed oil—avoid olive oil or butter, since they will burn at the temperatures required for frying.

✓ The flour coating provides a delicious crispy texture, protects the fish from soaking up too much oil, and also keeps the fillet in one piece. [4]

PASTA & SAUCES

INTRODUCTION TO PASTA

My paternal grandfather was a Sicilian immigrant who came to this country and opened up his own shoe business just before the Depression. He could make shoes from scratch or repair them. Once the Depression hit, he had to close his shop and work at one of the many shoe factories we had in Brockton, Massachusetts.

His downsizing meant that his little family ate a lot of pasta. My dad said they had pasta daily, just with a few different things but rarely meat. One night they had it with peas, the next night with just butter. If my little grandpa (5 feet tall) saw how the fancy restaurants today charge $25 for a plate of pasta, he'd laugh like hell.

That said, it's delicious and economical however you make it. This chapter will just give you a few sauce recipes to go over whatever pasta you like. The unwritten rule, though, is that the wider the pasta noodle, the thicker the sauce. For example, angel hair could have just butter and lemon on it, whereas penne pasta could accommodate a thick vodka sauce. But it's your decision to do what you like.

There is chick pea or lentil pasta if you're health conscious. There's whole wheat pasta, gluten free, and the regular pastas. There's homemade pasta, which is a ton of work and will not be covered in this cookbook.

The advice is often to cook it "al dente" which means "to the teeth" or slightly chewy. I like it slightly overcooked, the way my Yankee mother made it. Hey, you're the cook.

Pasta 101:

1. Read the directions on the box. Thinner pasta like Angel Hair cooks faster.
2. Use a big, deep pot with a lot of water. Pasta needs room to swim.
3. Bring the water to a ROLLING BOIL *first* before putting in the pasta. That means big bubbles breaking the surface. Start your timer from that point.
4. Drain well in a colander.

FUNNY STORY ALERT: My late mother-in-law, of whom I was very fond, failed to drain the pasta well. She didn't use a colander, but just scooped the pasta out of the water and plunked it on a plate, put the sauce on it, then handed it to my husband who was sitting on the other side of the table. Unfortunately, she handed it to him at an angle, with the contents of the plate sliding onto his lap. He kept his calm and simply said, "Hey, thanks, Mom."

ALFREDO SAUCE

★ EASY

You can make this rich by adding more butter or using real cream. Or make it lower calorie by using skim milk or evaporated skim milk. The flour/butter used at the beginning will make it a decently thick sauce whichever you decide.

INGREDIENTS:

1 T. butter

1 T. flour

1 cup milk, evaporated milk, half & half, or cream

¼ cup Parmesan cheese

¼ cup cream cheese

¼ tsp. ground nutmeg

Salt & pepper to taste

DIRECTIONS:

1. In a **small saucepan**, combine butter and flour. Sauté for 60 seconds.
2. **Whisk** in 1 cup of milk or cream. Cook till thick, stirring constantly.
3. Add Parmesan and cream cheese. Cook till melted and smooth.
4. Season with garlic powder, ground nutmeg, salt & pepper.
5. Serves 4.

———————

WHAT WE LEARNED:

✓ How to change a recipe to adjust for taste and calorie concerns.

✓ Nutmeg gives a distinctive flavor, but a little goes a long way. Taste!

★

TOMATO SAUCE

★ **EASY** – makes a bit of a mess, but it's still easy

Your neighbor kindly brings over a basket of tomatoes. You know you can't eat that many salads even if you're on a diet. What to do? Time to make the tomato sauce.

INGREDIENTS:

6 to 8 fresh tomatoes

One 6 oz. can tomato paste (save the can)

2 stalks celery with leaves – *diced*

½ cup green pepper – *diced*

½ cup onion – *diced*

1 tsp. dried basil

1 tsp. dried oregano

Garlic powder

2 T. sugar

Salt & pepper

DIRECTIONS:

1. Boil water in a **medium saucepan**. Using **tongs**, dip tomatoes in for about 30 seconds.
2. Peel skin off tomato and discard skin. It should come right off with your fingers.
3. Chop tomatoes coarsely.
4. Put all ingredients in **2-quart saucepan** with (3) 6 oz. cans (from the tomato paste you just used) of water.
5. Bring to a boil, then simmer about 45 minutes.
6. Add more spices, sugar, or garlic/garlic powder to taste.
7. Enjoy having your house smell like a fine Italian restaurant.

WHAT WE LEARNED:

✓ You can always freeze what you don't eat right away. Freeze in pint containers or whatever you'd normally finish in one meal, to make thawing easier. Tomato sauce is acidic and keeps fairly well.

★

LISA'S VODKA SAUCE – Stovetop

★ EASY

This is so delicious and is as professional as the $8 jars you see in gourmet shops.

INGREDIENTS:

2 T. olive oil

1 small onion – *diced*

2 slices prosciutto – *diced*

2 cloves garlic OR ½ tsp. garlic powder

1 large can crushed tomatoes (I like San Marzano)

¼ to ½ cup vodka

1 T. white sugar

1 tsp. salt

2 T parsley – *chopped*

½ cup heavy cream

DIRECTIONS:

1. Heat olive oil in **large skillet** 60 seconds. Add chopped onion and prosciutto and sauté till tender, about 5 minutes.
2. Add garlic; sauté another 2 minutes.
3. Add tomatoes, vodka, sugar, and salt and simmer for 15 minutes.
4. Add chopped parsley.
5. Cook and stir till thickened, another 15 minutes.
6. Lastly, stir in heavy cream and simmer till sauce thickens, about 5 minutes.

WHAT WE LEARNED:

✓ Most, but not all, of the vodka's alcohol will cook out or evaporate.[5]

✓ The vodka brings out the flavor of the tomatoes.

HERB BUTTER

★ EASY

This is great on pasta if you want something really simple like my Sicilian grandparents ate, or you could put it on potatoes, rice, fish, or veggies.

INGREDIENTS:

1 stick unsalted butter - *softened*

2 tsp. fresh parsley – *minced*

2 tsp. garlic powder

1 tsp. onion powder

2 tsp. dried tarragon

1 T. fresh chives – *minced fine*

½ tsp. salt

1/8 tsp. pepper

DIRECTIONS:

1. In a **small bowl**, combine all ingredients, mixing well.
2. Place mixture on a piece of **plastic wrap**, and roll it to form a smooth log. Twist the ends.
3. Refrigerate until firm.

WHAT WE LEARNED:

✓ You're already thinking of how you could change up the spices, aren't you?

✓ Italian seasoning, dill, Mexican spices . . . the possibilities are endless

QUICK CHEDDAR CHEESE SAUCE

★ **RIDICULOUSLY EASY**

INGREDIENTS:

½ cup mayonnaise

1/3 cup milk

1 cup cheese – *shredded*

DIRECTIONS:

1. In **small saucepan**, combine mayonnaise and milk. Cook on LOW HEAT about 5 minutes or until mixture thickens slight, stirring constantly.
2. Add cheese. Stir and heat just until cheese is melted. If it's too thick, add more milk, which you may have to do to any leftover sauce.
3. Serve over veggies, pasta, or toast.

MISCELLANEOUS SAUCES

PINEAPPLE-RAISIN SAUCE FOR HAM OR PORK - stovetop

★ MODERATELY EASY

INGREDIENTS:

1 cup raisins

1 cup water

2/3 cup of pineapple preserves

¼ cup butter (half a stick)

1 T. lemon juice

½ cup water

4 tsp. cornstarch

DIRECTIONS:

1. In **heavy 1-quart saucepan**, combine raisins and 1 cup water. Cook over MEDIUM HEAT until raisins are tender and most of the water is absorbed, about 15 minutes.
2. Add pineapple preserves, butter and lemon juice.
3. In **small bowl** combine water and cornstarch; stir until smooth.
4. Add cornstarch mixture to raisin-pineapple mixture; mix well.
5. Cook over MEDIUM HEAT, stirring frequently, until mixture begins to boil. Boil 1 minute, stirring constantly until mixture is thickened.
6. Yield: 2 cups. Serve over ham steak or pork chops

★

PHILLY CREAM CHEESE CHIVE SAUCE - Stovetop

★ EASY

INGREDIENTS:

One 8-oz. package cream cheese – *cubed*

½ cup milk

1 T. fresh chives – *chopped*

1 tsp. lemon juice

¼ tsp. garlic powder

Salt to taste

DIRECTIONS:

1. In **medium saucepan**, stir cream cheese and milk over LOW HEAT until smooth.
2. Stir in chives, lemon juice, garlic powder and salt.

WHAT WE LEARNED:

✓ How to dress up baked potatoes, green beans, broccoli or other vegetables.

✓ Don't be afraid to substitute scallions if you don't have chives.

★

ORIENTAL MARINADE

★ EASY

INGREDIENTS:

1 T. fresh ginger – *chopped* OR 2 tsp. dried ginger OR 1 tsp. ginger paste

2 cloves garlic – *finely chopped* OR 1 tsp. garlic powder

1 medium onion – *finely chopped*

2 T. sugar

1 cup soy sauce

½ cup sherry or other sweet wine

DIRECTIONS:

1. In a **medium-sized bowl** mix all ingredients and use for marinating beef, pork, or chicken.
2. Put a **plate** with meat on it inside a **tight-closing resealable bag**. Stick your bowl inside the bag and pour marinade over meat. Marinade for as long as you have—1 hour or overnight—you decide. Turn it over to the other side at least once during the marinating time.
3. Whatever marinade is left on the plate, use when you cook the meat. Discard what you don't use in cooking (food safety issue).

WHAT WE LEARNED:

✓ You may not need to use all the marinade you made.

✓ Remember, if raw meat touched *any* of the leftover marinade, you must discard it. If it didn't touch any of it, refrigerate for future use.

★

VELOUTÉ SAUCE FOR CHICKEN – stovetop/double boiler

★ EASY

INGREDIENTS:

2 T. butter

2 T. flour

2 cups chicken stock

Cream to taste

Seasoning to taste

DIRECTIONS:

1. In top of **double boiler**, melt the butter.
2. **Whisk** in flour. Mix well and cook for a few minutes.
3. Add the chicken stock. Stir over LOW HEAT until blended.
4. Simmer for 1 hour or until thick. Add a few tablespoons of cream at a time till it's how you like it. Season to taste. Thyme is nice with this sauce.
5. If not thick enough, make a paste with cornstarch and water, then add to sauce and cook till it's thick.

WHAT WE LEARNED:

✓ A double boiler cooks evenly and gently using steam. Pour 2 inches of water in the bottom. Put the top pan on and your ingredients. Simmer over LOW HEAT.

✓ Velouté means "velvety" in French. This is a great sauce for chicken croquettes.

YOGURT SAUCE

★ EASY

INGREDIENTS:

1 cup (8 oz.) Greek-style PLAIN yogurt

2 T. fresh mint leaves – *finely chopped* OR 1 tsp. dried mint

2 T. extra virgin olive oil

2 T. lime juice (about 1large lime)

½ tsp. salt

1 garlic clove OR ½ tsp. garlic powder

OPTIONAL: Diced cucumber and 1 tsp. dried dill for a Tzatziki sauce

DIRECTIONS:

1. In **medium mixing bowl**, whisk together all ingredients. Taste and adjust salt and lime juice if you like more.
2. Cover and refrigerate leftovers for up to 5 days. Put tape on the container with the date you made it.

WHAT WE LEARNED:

✓ How to expand our eating repertoire for a Middle East flavor.

✓ This sauce is great with grilled chicken, fish, lamb or vegetables.

★

STARCH – RICE & POTATOES

<u>ROAST POTATOES</u> – Preheat oven to 425°F

★ **RIDICULOUSLY EASY**

INGREDIENTS:

4 potatoes – *raw, cubed*

3 T. olive oil

½ tsp. dried rosemary

1 tsp. dried thyme

1 tsp. black pepper

½ tsp. salt

DIRECTIONS:

1. Cut up potatoes in quarters.
2. In a **medium-sized mixing bowl**, mix olive oil and spices.
3. Add potatoes to mixing bowl and toss to coat with the spiced oil.
4. Put all in a **baking pan** (sides not too high) and roast for 45 minutes or until fork inserted comes out easily. Potatoes will be slightly browned on the outside and tender inside.

NOTE: This is a great recipe when you're busy with other parts of the meal. It only takes a few minutes. You just pop in the oven, then go relax for a while.

DAY BEFORE MASHED POTATOES

★ MODERATELY EASY

We don't often have mashed potatoes because we're busy and there is a bit of elbow grease and cleanup with this dish. But if you are having folks over the next day, you don't want to be messing with this. Instead, make this ahead, then all you have to do is plop it in the oven and bake. This ensures that it will be hot enough, as it is a dense dish.

INGREDIENTS:

9 potatoes – *peeled & cubed* (Yukon Gold is preferred)

6 oz. (3/4 cup) chive cream cheese

1 cup sour cream

1 tsp. onion powder

1 tsp. salt

½ tsp. ground black pepper

2 T. butter

½ cup whipping cream

DIRECTIONS:

1. Put potatoes in **large pot** of COLD salted water to cover potatoes. BRING TO A BOIL, THEN LOWER TO SIMMER; cook till fork tender, about 15 minutes. Drain.
2. Transfer potatoes to a **large bowl**. Mash till smooth.
3. Mix into the bowl the remaining ingredients.
4. Cover; refrigerate overnight or a few hours if baking later that day.
5. Preheat oven to 350°F. LIGHTLY GREASE a **9" x 13" baking dish**.
6. Spread mixture in dish. Using a knife, make little whipped up waves on top.
7. Bake about 30 minutes. Will be hot and top will sport a nice crust.

WHAT WE LEARNED:

✓ How to plan ahead.

✓ Diced potatoes cook faster than whole potatoes.

★

RICKY'S FRENCH FRIES

★ MODERATELY EASY

I never had homemade French fries till my husband surprised me with these many years ago. He is the Fry King. As with any hot-oil frying, take care, monitor the cooking and don't walk away.

INGREDIENTS:

1 potato per person – all-purpose or baking potato

Vegetable oil – enough to fill a FryDaddy®

DIRECTIONS:

1. Slice potato with a **French fry cutter** if you have one. If not, slice how you like them (thin rounds for homemade potato chip-style or traditional lengthwise.)
2. Soak potatoes in **bowl** of cold water to cover for just a few minutes. Drain thoroughly and pat dry <u>thoroughly</u>.
3. Preheat **FryDaddy®** for 10 minutes. Oil must be hot.
4. Put in potatoes carefully with a **long slotted spoon** and cook till as brown as you like, about 10 minutes. Remove with **long slotted spoon**. Drain on a **bowl lined with newspaper or brown grocery bag paper** to soak up grease. Salt and pepper the fries.

WHAT WE LEARNED:

✓ French fry cutters are widely available at specialty kitchen stores.

✓ Soaking potatoes briefly in cold water removes starch and keeps your cooked fries from sticking together.

✓ Potatoes should be pat dry <u>thoroughly</u>. Wet potatoes into hot oil can cause dangerous splattering.

✓ Most of these small fryers, by design, do not reach the temperatures of a commercial fryolator; therefore, longer times are usually necessary.

★

DELMONICO POTATOES – Preheat oven to 400°F. Serves 6 to 8.

★ ADVANCED

These potatoes were served at Jimmy's Harborside, on Northern Avenue, Boston, MA, many years ago. It brings back happy memories of celebrating life's milestones at this elegant restaurant when it was located on Boston Harbor. This recipe is a bit of work, but you will be elegant, too, if you serve them.

INGREDIENTS:

4 cups potatoes – *cooked & diced* (about 4 or 5 medium potatoes)

3 T. butter

2-1/2 T. flour

2 cups half & half

1 tsp. salt

½ tsp. ground black pepper

½ cup white cheddar cheese – *shredded*

¼ cup Parmesan cheese – *grated*

¼ cup yellow cheddar cheese – *shredded*

DIRECTIONS:

1. Put potatoes in **large pot** of COLD salted water to cover potatoes. BRING TO A BOIL, THEN LOWER TO SIMMER; cook till fork tender, about 15 minutes. Drain.
2. In a **5-quart saucepan** over MEDIUM HEAT, make a roux by melting butter and stirring in flour till mixture is blended and smooth. Cook 60 seconds.
3. Gradually stir in half & half, salt and pepper and stir again till well blended.
4. Reduce heat to LOW, add white cheddar and Parmesan, stirring constantly to keep consistency smooth.
5. Add the cooked, diced potatoes, folding in gently with a spatula till well covered. Cook over LOW HEAT for a few minutes. Do not allow to boil.
6. Remove from heat and place in GREASED **shallow 6" x 12" baking dish**. Sprinkle with yellow cheddar cheese and place in 400°F oven. Bake just till cheese melts.

COCONUT RICE

★ **EASY**

The original recipe I used for this was crazy. I had too many notes on it, which is a bad sign. So I re-wrote it. This is so easy, it's embarrassing.

INGREDIENTS:

1 cup long-grain rice, such as jasmine

2 cups water

1 T. sugar

¾ cup coconut milk OR 1 T. coconut oil – to taste

½ tsp. salt

DIRECTIONS:

1. Cook rice according to package directions.
2. When done, just add the coconut milk or oil, sugar and salt. You're done!

EVEN EASIER COCONUT RICE

INGREDIENTS:

90-second rice packet

DIRECTIONS:

1. Cook rice 90 seconds in microwave. Pour into a serving bowl.
2. Add coconut milk, starting with a few tablespoons. Taste. Adjust if necessary. Wow! Even faster!

NOTE: This is a great dish to accompany Chinese or Indian food.

★

SPRING GREEN RISOTTO - stovetop

★ ADVANCED

Like many of my recipes, it's not difficult, just time consuming. The risotto technique is to gradually add the stock to an absorbing rice—which MUST be Arborio rice—then stand over it like a sentry. That's why you don't see it on too many menus. But it is creamy and delicious. To make it a meal, just add some cooked chicken or shrimp and a pre-made salad and you're done. Now you're dining like a sophisticate.

INGREDIENTS:

2 t. olive oil

1 cup onion – *chopped*

1 cup **Arborio** rice

4 cups chicken stock

2 cups fresh spinach – *chopped*

3 T. fresh chives – *cut with scissors*

1 T. dried thyme

Salt & pepper

½ cup grated Parmesan

DIRECTIONS:

1. Heat oil in **3-quart heavy saucepan**. Add onion; cook on low till soft, 5 minutes.
2. Add rice. Stir and cook another 3 minutes.
3. Bring stock to a boil in *another* saucepan; reduce heat and keep at a simmer. This will be your "mother ship" from which you'll draw.
4. Slowly add 1 cup of hot stock to rice, stirring constantly, allowing rice to simmer. When stock has been absorbed, add another ½ cup of stock and allow to simmer, stirring well until it has been absorbed.
5. Add spinach, chives and thyme. Continue cooking, adding stock, half a cup at a time, stirring constantly till rice is creamy and just tender. Altogether, rice should cook for 25-30 minutes.
6. Stir in salt and pepper and Parmesan. Serve immediately. Yield: 4.

WHAT WE LEARNED:

✓ That you need to use the right type of rice to make this correctly.

✓ Patience.

✓ Planning ahead. You did set the table and pre-make the salad, right?

★

BROWN RICE RISOTTO - stovetop

★ MODERATELY EASY

This risotto is a bit different than the traditional risotto. Brown rice usually takes a long time to cook, but you can leave this recipe to cook on the stove without all the half-a-cup-of-stock at a time activity and you standing over it.

INGREDIENTS:

1 cup **long-grain brown rice**

1 T. butter

2-1/2 cups chicken stock

Salt & pepper

½ cup grated Parmesan

DIRECTIONS:

1. In **3-quart large saucepan**, bring chicken stock to a **boil**. Add butter.
2. Once butter is melted, stir in rice and REDUCE HEAT TO SIMMER.
3. COVER and cook 45-50 minutes. The rice should be moist.
4. Remove from heat and fluff with fork.
5. Stir in cheese, garnish with parsley and serve immediately. Makes 2-1/4 cups.

WHAT WE LEARNED:

✓ That even brown rice can taste good.

★

DAD'S PIGNOLI-NUT LEMON RICE

★ EASY

INGREDIENTS:

1 cup long-grain rice

2-1/2 cups water

1 T. fresh lemon peel - *blanched*

2 T. butter

1 tsp. salt

2 T. butter

½ cup pignoli nuts (aka "pine nuts")

¼ cup fresh lemon juice

DIRECTIONS:

1. In **small saucepan**, blanch the lemon peel in rapidly boiling water for 5 minutes. Drain.
2. In **heavy 2-quart saucepan**, place 2 T. butter, 1 tsp. salt, then rice. Add 2-1/2 cups of water. BRING TO A BOIL, THEN LOWER HEAT TO SIMMER.
3. Cook COVERED about 20 minutes, till most moisture evaporates.
4. Meanwhile melt 2 T. butter in **heavy small skillet** over LOW heat.
5. Add pine nuts, lemon peel, and lemon juice to small skillet. Stir until heated through.
6. Pour over rice and cook another 5 minutes or until rice is tender. Fluff with fork.

WHAT WE LEARNED:

✓ How to cook conventional rice.

LOBSTER MACARONI AND CHEESE – Preheat oven to 350°F and stovetop

★ **MODERATELY EASY**

INGREDIENTS:

16 oz. pkg. elbow macaroni

Lobster meat OR 2 cups lobster bisque

2 T. butter

1 small onion – *diced*

1 cup milk – adjust if necessary

5 T. butter

5 T. flour

1 lb. Gruyere cheese – *shredded*

1 cup grated Romano cheese

3 cups cheddar – *shredded*

3 T. panko bread crumbs

1 T. butter - *melted*

Salt & pepper to taste

DIRECTIONS:

1. Cook pasta according to pkg. directions. Drain. Rinse with cold water to cool.
2. Melt 2 T. butter in a **large saucepan** over MEDIUM HEAT. Stir in onion, cook till soft about 5 minutes. Take out of pan and set aside.
3. Melt 5 T. butter in the same saucepan over MEDIUM HEAT. Whisk in flour, cook, about 1-2 minutes. Whisk 1 cup milk into the roux, bringing to simmer over MEDIUM HEAT. Cook till smooth.
4. Stir 3 cheeses into thickened milk mixture till melted. Season with salt & pepper. Add onions, lobster or lobster bisque, and macaroni.
5. Put mixture into a GREASED **4-quart casserole** OR GREASED **9" x 12" pan.** Bake 30 minutes.
6. Mix panko crumbs with 1 T. melted butter. Take pan out of oven and top with buttered crumbs and bake another 10 minutes. Yield: 8

WHAT WE LEARNED:

✓ How to make an executive decision to adjust the ingredients as necessary. How does it taste? How does it look? Adjust as needed.

VEGETABLES

MARY'S FRIED ZUCCHINI - stovetop

★ **EASY**

My late mother-in-law used to fry these up often. They are crispy and delicious and may be a good way to get vegetables into people who don't like them. Serve with ranch dressing on the side if you like.

INGREDIENTS:

1 medium fresh zucchini

¼ cup half & half

½ cup dried breadcrumbs – plain or Italian

Seasoning of your choice

Oil for frying

DIRECTIONS:

1. Slice zucchini evenly into ¼" rounds.
2. Set out **two shallow bowls**: Into the first one put the half & half. Into the 2nd one put the dried bread crumbs.
3. Dip rounds into half & half, then crumbs.
4. Heat a **large skillet** over medium heat for 60 seconds.
5. Add oil of your choice—olive, peanut, or canola oil—and heat for 60 seconds.
6. Carefully place each round into the oil. Don't crowd the pan.
7. Fry till golden, then turn over. DON'T WALK AWAY. First side cooks in about 3 minutes and the same for the second side.
8. Place completed zucchini on a paper towel lined platter and serve hot.

NOTE: Try different seasonings, like Cajun, onion powder, dill, Adobo.

ALICE'S STUFFED ZUCCHINI – Preheat oven to 350°F

★ **MODERATELY EASY**

INGREDIENTS:

3 medium sized zucchini

4 cups (small box) Ritz crackers – *crushed in a resealable bag*

1 stick butter - *melted*

½ tsp. garlic powder

½ onion – *minced*

2 T. parmesan

1 egg - *beaten*

Salt & pepper

DIRECTIONS:

1. In a **large pot**, put WHOLE zucchini and cover with COLD water. Bring to a boil and boil for 10 minutes. This is called parboiling (partial boiling)
2. Take out zucchini and cut in half LENGTHWISE.
3. Scoop out insides with a **grapefruit spoon** and place insides in a **mixing bowl**.
4. Lay zucchini "boats" into a GREASED **baking dish**.
5. Into the mixing bowl add the remaining ingredients to the insides and mix well.
6. Stuff shells with filling. Try using a **small ice cream scoop**. Mound it neatly.
7. Bake at 350°F for 40 minutes or until stuffing is golden brown.

WHAT WE LEARNED:

✓ What parboiling is. This gives the recipe a head start. Baking finishes it.

ZUCCHINI CASSEROLE – Preheat oven to 350°F

★ **EASY**

INGREDIENTS:

4 medium zucchini – *sliced into ½ thick rounds, then quarters (bite sized)*

¾ cup fresh carrot – *shredded*

½ medium onion – *diced*

6 T. butter - divided

2-1/4 cup herbed stuffing mix or croutons – *crushed in a resealable bag*

1 can condensed cream of chicken soup

½ cup sour cream

DIRECTIONS:

1. In a **large skillet**, melt 4 tablespoons of butter, then sauté zucchini, carrot and onion for about 5 minutes.
2. GREASE a **1-1/2 quart casserole dish.**
3. Melt remaining 2 T. butter and place in a **medium-sized mixing bowl**; add stuffing. Mix well.
4. Put half of the buttered stuffing in with the sautéed vegetables. Mix well.
5. Put vegetable mixture into casserole. Top with remaining stuffing.
6. Bake at 350°F UNCOVERED for 30-40 minutes. Serves 6.

LIN'S RATATOUILLE – Stovetop

★ EASY

This is something you can just throw together. Typically, ratatouille has eggplant in it. Put in if you like. If you don't have any, make it this way. Put in mushrooms if you like. This is an attractive and colorful side dish. Serve in little bowls.

INGREDIENTS:

1 Medium sized fresh zucchini – *cut into bite sized pieces*

1 Medium sized fresh summer squash (yellow) – *cut into bite sized pieces*

¼ onion – *chopped*

½ can diced tomatoes OR stewed tomatoes

1 tsp. oregano, basil or Italian seasoning

Salt & pepper to taste

Olive oil for frying

DIRECTIONS:

1. Heat a **large saucepan** over MEDIUM heat for 60 seconds. Add olive oil. Heat for another 60 seconds.
2. Add the two squashes and onion. Sauté till tender, about 5-10 minutes.
3. Add tomatoes and seasonings; heat through. You're done!

NOTE: FEEL FREE TO change the amounts of any of the ingredients to your liking. It always comes out good. Now you're a cook!

BRANDIED SWEET POTATOES – Stovetop

★ MODERATELY EASY

INGREDIENTS:

3 lbs. sweet potatoes

½ cup brown sugar

¼ cup brandy or other sweet liquor

2 T. butter

¼ tsp. ground cinnamon

¼ tsp. allspice

¼ cup pecans – *coarsely chopped, toasted*

DIRECTIONS:

1. Scrub potatoes. Cut into quarters. Place in **large pot**, cover with COLD WATER.
2. Boil with the skins on for 45 minutes or till tender (fork comes out easily).
3. Remove from pot. Pull off skins (should come off easily).
4. Mash sweet potatoes by hand or puree <u>briefly</u> in **food processor**. Put in a **serving bowl** and keep warm.
5. In **small saucepan** over MEDIUM HIGH HEAT, cook brown sugar, brandy, butter and spices for 5 minutes. Pour over mashed sweet potatoes.
6. Serve with toasted pecans if desired.

WHAT WE LEARNED:

✓ Remembered to scrub potatoes like I instructed you in the Food Safety chapter.

✓ That peeling a sweet potato is a challenge; that's why we do it this way here.

✓ If you puree potatoes in a food processor, BRIEFLY is key, like literally 3 seconds. Otherwise the texture gets weird.

✓ That you read the recipe through before trying it.

★

BUTTERSCOTCH YAMS – Preheat oven to 325°F

★ EASY

This recipe has corn syrup in it, which is basically pure sugar in syrup form.

FUNNY STORY ALERT: A friend of ours hosted a teenage guest who was in town to play in the Cape Cod Baseball league for a summer season. This young man and his pal decided to cook fish in the oven. So they took our friend's best cookie sheet and, thinking it was oil, poured corn syrup all over the cookie sheet and baked the fish in it. Good thing our friend was a firefighter. He came home to smoke alarms going off, burned fish and a ruined cookie sheet. Corn syrup may look like oil, but it's not. Pure sugar will get hot really fast, solidify, then burn. 'Nuff said.

INGREDIENTS:

2 cans (17 oz. each) yams – *well drained*

½ cup Karo® light or dark corn syrup

½ cup firmly packed brown sugar

¼ cup heavy cream or half & half

2 T butter

½ tsp. salt

½ tsp. cinnamon

REGULAR OVEN DIRECTIONS:

1. Arrange yams in single layer in GREASED **9" x 13" x 2"** baking dish. Bake at 325°F for 15 minutes.
2. In **heavy 2-quart saucepan**, combine remaining ingredients, stirring constantly. Bring to boil over MEDIUM HEAT and boil 5 minutes.
3. Pour sauce over yams. Bake, basting frequently, another 15 minutes or till glazed.

MICROWAVE DIRECTIONS:

1. In **3-quart microproof baking dish**, combine all sauce ingredients.
2. Microwave on HIGH, stirring once, for 3-4 minutes.
3. Add yams, toss to coat well.
4. Microwave on HIGH, basting once, 6 more minutes or till glazed.

WHAT WE LEARNED:

✓ What corn syrup is.

✓ Basting – just take a big spoon, scoop up the sauce, and pour over the item.

★

ZIPPY GREEN BEANS – Stovetop

★ RIDICULOUSLY EASY

INGREDIENTS:

1 can kitchen sliced green beans

1 T. butter

1 tsp. maple mustard OR 1 tsp. regular mustard + 1 tsp. maple syrup

½ tsp. dried dill OR lemon dill seasoning

DIRECTIONS:

1. Heat green beans thoroughly (microwave or stovetop); drain.
2. Place in **serving bowl**.
3. Dump in butter, mustard, and dill and mix well.

★

<u>**3 BEAN SALAD**</u> – Refrigerate overnight

★ **RIDICULOUSLY EASY**

This recipe keeps well and is the perfect addition for a picnic.

INGREDIENTS:

1 can yellow wax beans - *drained*

1 can green beans - *drained*

½ can red kidney beans - *drained*

1 small can mushrooms – *drained*

DRESSING INGREDIENTS:

¼ cup lemon juice

½ cup wine vinegar

½ tsp. salt

½ tsp. pepper

½ tsp. garlic powder

3 packets of artificial sweetener OR 2 T. white sugar

DIRECTIONS:

1. Drain beans and mushrooms in a **colander**. Place in a **bowl with cover**.
2. Make dressing. Pour over beans and mushrooms.
3. Refrigerate overnight so all the flavors can meld together.

OVEN-ROASTED VEGETABLES

★ EASY

INGREDIENTS:

2 lbs. assorted fresh vegetables – *thickly sliced*:

Eggplant

Zucchini

Summer squash

Large mushrooms

Red onion

Red, green, or yellow bell peppers

¾ cup Italian or olive oil vinaigrette dressing

DIRECTIONS:

1. Cut up vegetables in thick slices or chunks.
2. In **large shallow glass baking dish** or **plastic bag**, toss vegetables with dressing.
3. Cover or close bag and marinate in refrigerator, turning once, up to 1 hour.
4. Preheat oven to 425°F.
5. Remove vegetables from refrigerator, and pour all into an UNGREASED **METAL roasting pan.**
6. Roast 20 minutes or till vegetables are tender, stirring once.

WHAT WE LEARNED:

✓ You don't need to grease the baking dish because you've got a lot of oil, which will be enough to keep things from sticking.

✓ In general, don't use glass or ceramic in temperatures higher than 425°F. So if you're in a pinch and need to use glass or ceramic cookware for recipes that call for baking *pans*, reduce the baking temperature by about 25°F. Some glassware such as Pyrex[1] can be prone to thermal shock, meaning rapid change in temperature

---

1. https://www.consumerreports.org/consumerist/
why-pyrex-bowls-explode/#_853ae90f0351324bd73ea615e6487517__4c761f170e016836ff84498202b99827__853ae90f0351324bd73ea615e6487517_text_43ec3e5dee6e706af7766fffea512721_Pyrex_0bcef9c45bd8a48eda1b26eb0c61c869_20is_0bcef9c45bd8a48eda1b26eb0c61c869_20made_0bcef9c45bd8a48eda1b26eb0c61c869_20of_0bcef9c45bd8a48eda1b26eb0c61c869_20glass._6cff047854f19ac2aa52aac51bf3af4a_text_43ec3e5dee6e706af7766fffea512721_The_0bcef9c45bd8a48eda1b26eb0c61c869_20text_0bcef9c45bd8a48eda1b26eb0c61c869_20book_0bcef9c45bd8a48eda1b26eb0c61c869_20definition_0bcef9c45bd8a48eda1b26eb0c61c869_20of_c0cb5f0fcf239ab3d9c1fcd31fff1efc_by_0bcef9c45bd8a48eda1b26eb0c61c869_20different_0bcef9c45bd8a48eda1b26eb0c61c869_20amounts_0bcef9c45bd8a48eda1b26eb0c61c869_2C_0bcef9c45bd8a48eda1b26eb0c61c869_20causing_0bcef9c45bd8a48eda1b26eb0c61c869_20stress.

could cause your bakeware to shatter. Make sure your dishes are completely cool before refrigerating or freezing them. Or if you've got a breakfast casserole[2] chilling overnight, allow it to come closer to room temperature before popping it in the oven.[6]

★

2. https://www.bhg.com/recipes/breakfast/casseroles/easy-breakfast-casseroles/?

<u>COMFORT CARROTS</u> – Stovetop and food processor

★ **MODERATELY EASY**

INGREDIENTS:

2 lbs. fresh carrots – *peeled and cut into 1-inch chunks*

1 vanilla bean OR 1 tsp. vanilla extract

2 T. unsalted butter – *room temperature*

2/3 cup light cream

1 T. grainy mustard, like Dijon

2 T. fresh chives – *cut with scissors* (save some for garnish)

½ tsp. grated nutmeg

Salt and pepper to taste

DIRECTIONS:

1. If using a vanilla bean, lay on a **cutting board** and split lengthwise with a **sharp knife**. Place the carrots and vanilla bean in a **saucepan** and cover generously with water. Bring to a boil, then simmer UNCOVERED till carrots are tender, about 15-20 minutes. Fork should go in and out of carrot easily.
2. Drain well and discard the vanilla bean.
3. Place carrots in a **food processor**. Add butter and process to a smooth puree.
4. With the machine running, slowly pour the cream through the feed tube and process till completely blended.
5. Add mustard, chives, nutmeg, salt and pepper. Process JUST till combined.
6. Serve immediately or gently reheat in a double boiler over simmering water at serving time. Garnish with snipped chives. Makes 6-8 servings.

WHAT WE LEARNED:

✓ That real vanilla beans are about $20 a jar. FYI, by splitting the bean, you are exposing all the lovely, expensive vanilla seeds inside to envelop the food. You may want to try this recipe with the more affordable extract or even imitation vanilla extract to see how you like it.

ROASTED CARROTS – Preheat oven to 425°F

★ **RIDICULOUSLY EASY** - These are so delicious, they're like candy.

INGREDIENTS:

Part 1: 10 medium carrots – peeled and cut into even sizes

2 T. olive oil

Salt & pepper

1-1/2 tsp. dried thyme

Part 2:

½ tsp. dried cumin

½ tsp. dried coriander

2 T. unsalted butter – room temperature

½ tsp. turmeric powder

2 T. fresh mint – chopped OR 2 tsp. dried mint

DIRECTIONS:

1. Place carrot pieces in a **large bowl** and toss with olive oil, salt & pepper, and thyme.
2. Heat a **heavy baking sheet** in the 425°F oven for 3-4 minutes. Remove from the oven and place the carrots on it in one layer.
3. Roast carrots for 20-25 minutes, stirring the carrots every 10 minutes. They should be caramelized and tender when done.
4. While the carrots are in the oven, make Part 2 by combining all ingredients in your **serving bowl**.
5. Remove the carrots from the oven when done and add to serving bowl. Toss all ingredients together well. Serve immediately. Yield: 6.

WHAT WE LEARNED:

✓ That things should be cut to uniform size for even cooking. You don't want one mushy carrot and one hard carrot. All should cook evenly.

★

CAULIFLOWER RISOTTO

★ EASY

Not too many people get excited about cauliflower. But this dish is delicious and tastes like a traditional risotto.

INGREDIENTS:

2 cups fresh cauliflower

1 T. olive oil

1 T. onion – *chopped*

½ cup vegetable broth – use the paste

2 T. heavy cream (OR if you don't have heavy cream, use 2 T melted butter and 1/3 cup of milk)

2 T. fresh parsley – *chopped*

½ cup grated Parmesan

DIRECTIONS:

1. Put cauliflower in **food processor**. Pulse till they it's the size of grains of rice.
2. In a **large skillet** over MEDIUM HEAT, cook onion in olive oil till tender, about 5 minutes.
3. Add cauliflower to skillet and toss to coat. Add vegetable broth and cook till tender, about 10 minutes.
4. Add cream, parsley, and Parmesan.
5. Season with salt & pepper to taste.

★

<u>MUSHROOMS IN SOUR CREAM</u> – Stovetop

★ EASY

A word about fresh mushrooms. Some advice is that they shouldn't be washed, but merely brushed with a mushroom brush to get off the dirt. Many of the rest of us don't subscribe to that. Mushrooms are grown in compost, along with sand and dirt, which clings to them. A few rogue cooks and I suggest the following. **Rinse them off quickly in cold water. Don't soak, as they absorb water. Pat them dry.**

INGREDIENTS:

3 T. butter

½ cup onion – *chopped*

1 lb. fresh mushrooms – *sliced*

1 cup sour cream

¼ tsp. salt

Pinch pepper

1 T. parsley

DIRECTIONS:

1. Melt butter in **large skillet**.
2. Add onion. Sauté till tender, about 5 minutes.
3. Add mushrooms and sauté, about 4 minutes, stirring constantly.
4. Remove from heat and add sour cream, salt & pepper, and parsley.
5. Serve on toast or as a side dish.

WHAT WE LEARNED:

✓ How to deal with mushroom-washing protocol.

★

MRS. STONE'S STUFFED MUSHROOMS – Stovetop & Preheat oven to 375°F

★ MODERATELY EASY

The tricky part is mounding the stuffing into the cap. There will be spillover. Don't worry about it. Someone will eat the crispy bits.

INGREDIENTS:

1 lb. fresh mushrooms - WHOLE

4 T. (half a stick) butter (or more if you wish)

¼ cup onion – *chopped fine*

½ tsp. garlic powder

½ tsp. each of salt and black pepper

1/3 cup fine dry breadcrumbs – plain or Italian

Paprika for sprinkling

DIRECTIONS:

1. Rinse mushrooms quickly in cold water. Don't soak. Pat them dry.
2. Separate the stem from the cap. Just pull the stem out, leaving the cap whole.
3. Put the caps on a **cookie sheet**, hollow side up.
4. Dice the stems fine, discarding any dried or woody parts.
5. In a **large skillet** melt butter, add onion and diced stems and sauté for about 5 minutes till onion is tender. Add spices.
6. Add breadcrumbs to skillet and stir well. This is your stuffing.
7. Using either a **small ice cream scoop** or an iced tea spoon, dig into the stuffing and place a spoonful into each mushroom cap.
8. Once you've done that, carefully flip the cap so the stuffing is on the bottom.
9. Dot each mushroom cap with a tiny bit of butter. Sprinkle with paprika.
10. Bake at 375°F for 20 minutes. Test one. Mushroom should be tender.

WHAT WE LEARNED:

✓ How to wow your friends with a complicated recipe. My dad always hated mushrooms till he tried these.

✓ Try different spices, adding crabmeat or bacon, etc.

★

MEMPHIS DRY-RUB MUSHROOMS[7] – Preheat oven to 400°F

★ EASY

This dish looks very strange while you're making it and it still looks strange when you serve it. Don't let that throw you. This is a savory and delicious dish. Be adventurous! Sometimes I don't have all the rub ingredients so I use what I have. It still turns out great.

RUB INGREDIENTS:

½ cup packed dark brown sugar

1 T. dried paprika

2 T. kosher salt (the large crystals)

2 T. onion powder

2 T. garlic powder

1 T. ground black pepper

1-1/2 tsp. dried cumin

1-1/2 tsp. dry mustard

MUSHROOM INGREDIENTS:

2 lbs. large mushrooms or Portobello – *sliced thickly*

½ cup canola oil or grapeseed oil

¼ cup Worcestershire sauce

DIRECTIONS:

1. Make the rub by combining all the ingredients. You probably won't use it all, so store in an **airtight container** for next time.
2. Rinse mushrooms quickly in cold water. Don't soak! Pat dry. Slice thickly.
3. Place mushrooms on a **large sheet pan** (low sides); drizzle with oil and Worcestershire.
4. Gently massage the dry rub into the mushrooms. (The oil will make it stick)
5. Roast mushrooms on top rack until deeply browned and crisp at the edges, about 25 minutes in convection oven.

WHAT WE LEARNED:

✓ What a dry rub is.

✓ That "packed" when referring to brown sugar means pressed tightly into the measuring cup, as opposed to loosely packed ingredients like flour.

SCALLOPED CORN SUPREME – Preheat oven to 350°F

★ **EASY**

INGREDIENTS:

One 15.25 oz. can creamed corn

1 cup milk

1 egg – *well beaten*

1 cup saltine crackers (30) – *crushed*

¼ cup onion – *minced*

3 T. chopped pimiento

¾ tsp. salt

Dash black pepper

TOPPING:

½ cup saltines (15) – *crushed*

1 T. butter – *melted*

———————————

DIRECTIONS:

1. In **medium saucepan**, combine corn and milk. Heat through.
2. Gradually stir in beaten egg, stirring constantly.
3. Add 1 cup cracker crumbs, onion, pimiento, salt & pepper; mix well.
4. Pour into GREASED **8" x 1-1/2" baking dish** or **pan**.
5. Combine topping ingredients; sprinkle over corn.
6. Bake at 350°F for 20 minutes. Yield: 6

WHAT WE LEARNED:

✓ That a beaten egg acts as a binder for the ingredients.

✓ That when you put beaten egg into a recipe, you should stir well until it's incorporated. You don't want bits of scrambled egg in it.

★

SWEET BOURBON CORN PUDDING - Preheat oven to 350°F

★ EASY

INGREDIENTS:

2 large eggs

¾ cup evaporated milk

One 15.25 oz. can of *creamed* corn

One 15.25 oz. can of *whole kernel* corn OR 2 cups fresh or frozen corn

2 T. unsalted butter – *melted*

½ tsp. ground nutmeg

¼ tsp. salt

1/8 tsp. black pepper

In a small bowl, mix:

3 T. cornstarch

2 T. bourbon

DIRECTIONS:

1. GREASE an **8" square baking dish** or **brownie pan**.
2. In a **large mixing bowl**, whisk together eggs and milk.
3. Add all remaining ingredients, including cornstarch/whiskey.
4. Pour into baking dish.
5. Bake 45 minutes or till lightly browned. Serve hot.

★

CHEESE CORN MEXICALI – Preheat oven to 350°F

★ **EASY**

INGREDIENTS:

1 T. butter

¼ cup onion – *chopped*

1 can whole kernel corn

½ cup sliced olives

2 T. flour

1/2 tsp. salt

¼ tsp. chili powder

Dash black pepper

1 cup cheddar cheese – *shredded*

1 small can tomato sauce

DIRECTIONS:

1. In **small skillet**, sauté onion in butter.
2. In a **large mixing bowl** combine remaining ingredients, including sautéed onion.
3. Turn into a BUTTERED **3-cup casserole dish**.
4. Sprinkle cheese on top. Pour tomato sauce over all.
5. Bake at 350°F for 25 minutes.

CREAMY CORN ITALIANO - Stovetop

★ EASY

INGREDIENTS:

2 T. butter

½ cup scallions – *sliced diagonally*

½ tsp. garlic powder

½ tsp. dried oregano

¼ tsp. dried basil

1 can cream of celery soup

2 cans (15.25 oz.) whole kernel corn – *drained*

¼ cup milk

½ cup diced tomatoes – *drained*

DIRECTIONS:

1. In **large saucepan**, sauté scallions in butter till tender. Add spices.
2. Add remaining ingredients. Heat through.

SOUPS, STEWS, AND CHOWDERS

TURKEY CROCKPOT CHILI – Stovetop and Crockpot

★ EASY

INGREDIENTS:

- 1-1/4 lbs. lean ground turkey
- 1 large onion – *chopped*
- 1 garlic clove – *minced* OR ½ tsp. garlic powder
- One 1.25 oz. envelope chili seasoning mix OR 1 tsp. Adobo

OR 1 tsp. cumin and 1 tsp. ground chili powder

One 12 oz. can beer

1-1/2 cups frozen whole corn kernels – I like the Super Sweet

1 red bell pepper – *chopped*

1 green bell pepper – *chopped*

One 28 oz. can <u>crushed</u> tomatoes

One 15 oz. can black beans – *drained and rinsed*

One 8-oz. can tomato sauce

<u>¾ tsp. salt</u>

TOPPINGS: shredded Cheddar or Monterey Jack, finely chopped red onion, sliced fresh jalapenos, shredded lettuce, sour cream, guacamole.

DIRECTIONS:

1. In a **large skillet**, cook first 4 ingredients over MEDIUM-HIGH HEAT, stirring often, for 8 minutes or till turkey crumbles and is no longer pink.
2. Stir in beer, and cook 2 minutes, stirring occasionally.
3. Spoon mixture into a **5-1/2 quart crockpot**.
4. Stir in corn and remaining ingredients till well blended.
5. Cover and cook on LOW for 6 hours.
6. Serve with desired toppings.

★

CREAMY TOMATO-BASIL SOUP – Stovetop and blender or immersion blender

★ **EASY**

INGREDIENTS:

2 T. olive oil

1-1/2 cups raw onion – *chopped*

1 cup vegetable broth

29 oz. can of diced tomatoes – *undrained*

1-1/2 cups (one 15-oz. can) canned Great Northern beans – *rinsed & drained*

½ tsp. kosher salt

½ cup fresh basil – *chopped* OR 2 tsp. dried basil OR 2 T. basil from jar

½ tsp. black pepper

DIRECTIONS:

1. In **medium saucepan** (**not** a non-stick if planning to use an immersion blender), over MEDIUM HIGH HEAT, warm oil. Add onion and cook till tender, about 5-8 minutes.
2. Add remaining ingredients. Increase heat to HIGH and bring to a boil. Cook 5 minutes.
3. Stir in basil. Pour into a **blender*** and puree till smooth. OR use an immersion blender by sticking right into the saucepan and blending till smooth.
4. Adjust seasonings if necessary. Yield: 4

WHAT WE LEARNED:

✓ Basil comes in many forms. If you can't find fresh and don't want to use dried basil, check out the produce section for the basil in a jar, which will keep for a few months in the refrigerator.

✓ Great Northern beans, a type of white bean, add body to this soup, thickening it without adding a lot of calories.

*NOTE: You could pour this into a food processor to puree, but it may leak and make a mess. I'd use the blender or immersion blender if available.

★

PAMMY'S GREEN SPLIT PEA SOUP WITH HAM – Stovetop and Crockpot

★ ADVANCED

This isn't actually difficult, but there are a lot of steps, hence the ADVANCED degree. This is a good recipe to make if you're home all day or snowed in. Start this bad boy early in the afternoon if you want it for supper.

INGREDIENTS:

8 cups water

1 large ham bone OR ham slice – *diced*

2 cups dried split green peas (or yellow for a milder flavor)

2 large fresh carrots – *peeled and diced*

2 onions – *chopped small*

2 large celery ribs, including leaves – *chopped*

2 tsp. beef bouillon paste OR 2 cubes

1 tsp. salt

¼ tsp. black pepper

½ tsp. pinch dried thyme

DIRECTIONS:

1. Rinse peas in cold water, inspect for bad ones, and add to **large stockpot**.
2. Add 8 cups of cold water to pot.
3. Bring to a boil. Remove from heat, COVER and let soak for 1 hour.
4. Return stockpot to stove and bring back to a boil.
5. Once it is boiling, you can continue cooking on the stove OR pour into a crockpot.
6. Add ham, carrots, onions, celery, beef bouillon paste, salt & pepper, thyme.
7. <u>If cooking on stove</u>: COVER and simmer for 1-1/2 hours.
8. <u>If cooking in **crockpot**:</u> cook on HIGH for 3 hours.
9. Remove ham bone (if used) and cut off any remaining ham into bite sized pieces and return to pot.
10. If you desire a thick soup, puree it in **blender** or with an immersion blender. OR just puree half, according to preference. Try adding ¼ teaspoon of Liquid Hickory Smoke for a smokey flavor or Andouille sausage instead of ham.

WHAT WE LEARNED:

✓ Split green peas need to be rinsed and inspected for small stones, shriveled peas or bits of soil.

✓ Soaking peas makes them more digestible (less gas) and speeds cooking time.

CREAM OF CARROT SOUP – Stovetop and Microwave

★ EASY

INGREDIENTS:

1 lb. fresh carrots (1 bag) – *peeled and sliced lengthwise*

Two 13-3/4 oz. cans chicken broth (about 3 cups)

3 T. flour

3 T. butter

1/3 cup half & half, cream, or milk – to taste

1 tsp. dill weed

¼ tsp. black pepper

½ tsp. salt

Sour cream for garnishing

Scallions for garnishing – *cut*

DIRECTIONS:

1. Put carrots in microwave with 1 cup of broth. Cook 12 minutes on HIGH or until soft.
2. Pureé cooked carrots in **food processor, blender**, or use an immersion blender.
3. Put mixture into **large saucepan** with remaining broth. Bring to a boil.
4. In a **small bowl**, mix 3 T. of butter with 3 T. of flour. Cook 60 seconds in **small frying pan**. Add to soup.
5. Cook soup for 1 minute on MEDIUM HIGH to thicken.
6. Add half & half, cream or milk. Heat gently till heated through.
7. Season with salt and pepper and dill. Serve with a dollop of sour cream.

WHAT WE LEARNED:

✓ The microwave is our friend when cooking dense vegetables like carrots.

✓ That we don't have to spend a lot of time chopping things small when they are going to be pureéd anyway.

★

BROCCOLI-CHEESE SOUP – Stovetop and Oven

★ EASY

This tastes as good as anything you get in those fancy restaurants for $7 a cup.

INGREDIENTS:

1 cup vegetable broth

1 cup cold milk } *Mix in a small bowl*

2 T. flour }

¼ tsp. kosher salt

Pinch cayenne pepper

2 cups *roasted* broccoli* - or if you're lazy, just microwave broccoli first.

2 T. uncooked scallions - cut

½ cup cheese – *shredded* – I like Cheddar

*TO ROAST BROCCOLI: Preheat oven to 425°F. Slice broccoli, toss with olive oil and salt. Lay flat on **cookie sheet**. Roast about 30 minutes or till tender.

DIRECTIONS:

1. In a **medium-sized saucepan**, whisk together broth, milk/flour combo, salt & cayenne pepper.
2. Cook over MEDIUM HIGH HEAT till thick and bubbly, about 4 minutes.
3. Stir in cooked/roasted broccoli and scallions.
4. Remove from heat and stir in cheese. YIELD: 2

NOTE: If broccoli is too chunky, pureé in food processor, blender, or immersion blender. OR pureé just part of it so it looks attractive with a few broccoli chunks.

<u>VINEYARD CLAM CHOWDER</u> – Stovetop

★ MODERATELY EASY

Being a long-time resident of Massachusetts, I treasure a good clam chowder. You can't get decent chowder in any state except Massachusetts and Maine. If you don't live in or near either of these two states, you can make your own. We love chowder so much we could have it intravenously injected. Carry on.

INGREDIENTS:

2 cans chopped clams – *save the broth!* OR fresh clams if you have them.

¼ lb. salt pork – *diced* OR fatty bacon - *diced*

1 medium onion – *chopped*

2 raw medium-sized potatoes – *diced*

2 cups (1 pint) light cream OR milk if watching calories

1 T. butter

3 T. flour } Mix together

3 T. butter }

Salt & pepper – to taste

DIRECTIONS:

1. In **large heavy saucepan**, cook the pork or bacon. Remove and set aside.
2. Sauté the chopped onion in the fat.
3. Add the saved broth, diced potatoes, and enough water to cover all by one inch.
4. Cook till potatoes are tender (not long because they're diced). Fork should go in and out easily.
5. Thicken the chowder with the roux of 3 T. butter and 3 T. flour. Cook for at least one minute or till thick.
6. In a **measuring cup**, melt butter in microwave, then add the cream. Add to chowder. Put the bacon or pork back in the chowder.
7. Add the clams last. (I chop them even finer in the **food chopper**.) They only need to be heated through. Serve chowder with oyster crackers.

WHAT WE LEARNED:

✓ Potatoes cook fast when cut small.

✓ Never, ever, overcook clams or you will have chewy "erasers" as my mother-in-law used to say.

★

CORN AND CRAB CHOWDER – Stovetop

★ MODERATELY EASY

INGREDIENTS:

1 T. olive oil

2 T. butter

2 all-purpose potatoes – *peeled & diced*

2 ribs celery – *chopped*

1 medium yellow onion – *chopped*

1 red bell pepper – *seeded & diced (make sure you cut away the ribs)*

1 T. Old Bay seasoning OR 1 T. seafood seasoning

3 T. flour

2 cups chicken broth

1 quart whole milk

3 cups corn kernels (1 package frozen)

8 oz. cooked lump crabmeat (a can or two – *drained*)

DIRECTIONS:

1. Heat a **stockpot** over MEDIUM HEAT for 60 seconds. Add olive oil and butter.
2. As you chop your vegetables, add to pot: potatoes, celery, onion, and bell pepper.
3. Add seasoning.
4. Sauté vegetables for 5 minutes, then sprinkle in flour. Cook and stir constantly for 2 minutes.
5. Stir in broth and combine.
6. Stir in milk and combine. Bring to a boil.
7. Add corn and crabmeat and SIMMER ON LOW for 5 minutes.
8. Adjust seasonings if necessary.

WHAT WE LEARNED:

✓ When you add flour to a dish, you must cook it at least 60 seconds. It's raw flour and must be cooked.

★

HAM-VEGETABLE CHOWDER - Stovetop

★ EASY

INGREDIENTS:

1 quart water (4 cups)

One 10-oz. package of frozen chopped broccoli

2 cups fully cooked smoked ham – *diced*

2 cups fresh carrots – *thinly sliced*

2 cups celery – *thinly sliced*

½ cup onion – *chopped*

½ tsp. salt

2 cups milk

½ cup Bisquick baking mix

8 oz. Swiss cheese – *diced* (about 2 cups)

DIRECTIONS:

1. In a **4-quart Dutch oven**, heat water, ham, broccoli, carrots, celery, onion, and salt to boiling. Reduce heat. COVER and SIMMER for 10 minutes.
2. In **small bowl** gradually stir milk into baking mix. Will be lumpy.
3. Pour into the pot. Heat to BOILING, stirring constantly, for one minute. Remove from heat.
4. Stir in Swiss cheese. Let stand till melted, about 5 minutes. YIELD: 6

ANDOUILLE CHOWDER – Stovetop

★ **EASY**

INGREDIENTS:

1 tsp. oil

1 large onion (about 1 cup) – *chopped*

3 sticks andouille sausage (about 2/3 lb.) – *skinned & sliced into bite-sized pieces*

3 medium potatoes (about 2-1/2 cups) – *diced small*

1-1/2 cups corn (frozen or canned – *drained*)

1 can chicken broth

1 can water

2 cups lowfat milk

2 T. cornstarch or flour }

3 T. milk } Mix in a small bowl

DIRECTIONS:

1. In **stockpot or large saucepan**, sauté onion and andouille lightly in oil. Do not brown. Add chicken broth, fill the can with water and add to pot.
2. Add cubed potatoes, COVER and simmer about 15 minutes or till potatoes are tender.
3. Add corn and milk and return to a boil.
4. Thicken to desired consistency with flour/milk mixture.

QUICK CHICKEN-CORN CHOWDER - Stovetop

★ EASY

INGREDIENTS:

1 cup cooked chicken – *diced*

2 cups white rice – *cooked*

4 T. butter (half a stick)

2/3 cup onion – *coarsely chopped*

½ cup green pepper – *coarsely chopped*

2 cups chicken stock

2 cans condensed cream of chicken soup

Two 14.75 oz. cans of creamed corn

5 cups milk

4 T. fresh parsley – *snipped*

¼ tsp. paprika

¼ tsp. salt

Black pepper to taste

DIRECTIONS:

1. Cook chicken ahead of time. If you have canned chicken, or leftover chicken from a grocery-store roasted chicken, that works also and is even faster.
2. Cook rice. If you are in a hurry, try using the 90-second rices instead.
3. In a **large saucepan**, melt butter over LOW HEAT. Add onion and green pepper and cook about 5 minutes until onion is golden.
4. Combine chicken stock with chicken soup and add to onion mixture.
5. Heat, stirring constantly, until smooth.
6. Add corn, cooked chicken, cooked rice, milk, parsley, and paprika. Heat thoroughly, stirring frequently.
7. Season with salt & pepper. YIELD: 8 servings

★

ZUCCHINI SOUP - Stovetop

★ EASY

This soup can be served hot or cold.

INGREDIENTS:

2 T. unsalted butter

1 T. olive oil

1 yellow onion – *finely chopped*

1-3/4 lb. zucchini (about 4 medium zucchini) – *sliced*

3-1/2 cups chicken stock

3 T. fresh oregano – *finely chopped* OR 2 tsp. dried oregano

½ tsp. salt

¼ tsp. finely ground pepper

½ cup whipping cream or plain yogurt

DIRECTIONS:

1. In a **3-quart saucepan**, heat butter and oil. Add onion and sauté over LOW HEAT, stirring occasionally, until translucent.
2. Add zucchini and continue sautéing for 2 minutes.
3. Add chicken stock and oregano and bring to a simmer. COVER and cook for 30 minutes or till tender.
4. Pureé soup in a **food processor, blender**, or use an immersion blender.
5. Return to saucepan. Add salt & pepper.
6. Add cream if serving hot.
7. If serving cold, bring soup to room temperature and whisk in plain yogurt.

<u>MUSHROOM MUSTARD SOUP</u> - Stovetop

★ EASY

This is an elegant addition to a steak dinner—either as a first course or a side dish.

INGREDIENTS:

1 stick butter

2 lbs. fresh mushrooms – *washed and thinly sliced*

4 cups chicken stock

½ cup dry sherry or other sweet wine

1 T. Dijon mustard

Salt & pepper

1 cup whipping cream

DIRECTIONS:

1. In **large heavy saucepan** over MEDIUM HIGH HEAT, melt butter.
2. Add mushrooms and cook until liquid evaporates, stirring frequently, about 10 minutes.
3. **Whisk** in chicken stock, wine, and mustard. Simmer for 10 minutes.
4. Season with salt & pepper.
5. Add whipping cream and warm through. DO NOT BOIL at this point.

WHAT WE LEARNED:

✓ When you add cream to a recipe, don't boil it. You can heat it well, but if you boil it, it may separate into chunks. Separation won't hurt you from a food safety perspective, but it will look unappetizing.

HUNGARIAN MUSHROOM SOUP – Stovetop

★ **MODERATELY EASY** - This recipe tastes just like the fancy ones in restaurants.

INGREDIENTS:

12 oz. (about 3-1/2 cups) fresh mushrooms – *rinsed and sliced*

2 cups onion – *chopped*

4 T. butter - divided

3 T. flour

1 cup milk

2-3 tsp. dried dill weed

1 T. Hungarian paprika

1 T. tamari (a Japanese variety of soy sauce)

2 tsp. fresh lemon juice

¼ cup fresh parsley – *chopped*

1 tsp. salt - or to taste

Ground black pepper – to taste

¼ cup sour cream

2 cups vegetable stock OR chicken stock - divided

DIRECTIONS:

1. **In large skillet**, melt 2 T. of butter and sauté onion for 2 minutes. Salt lightly. Add mushrooms, half of the dill, ½ cup of the stock, tamari, and paprika.
2. COVER and SIMMER 15 minutes.
3. **In large saucepan**, melt remaining butter. Whisk in flour and cook for 2 minutes, stirring constantly.
4. Add milk. Cook over LOW HEAT, stirring frequently, for 10 minutes, until thick.
5. Stir in mushroom mixture and remaining stock. COVER and SIMMER 10 minutes.
6. Just before serving, add salt, pepper, lemon juice, sour cream and, if desired, extra dill. Garnish with parsley. Soup will thicken upon standing.

WHAT WE LEARNED:

✓ Rinse fresh mushrooms quickly in cold water, don't soak, pat dry.

✓ *Divided* – means you will use this amount in several stages, not all at once.

HEARTY GUMBO – Stovetop

★ MODERATELY EASY

INGREDIENTS:

1 cup brown rice (or white if you prefer) – *cooked*

2 tsp. vegetable oil

2 T. flour

1 red pepper – *chopped*

1 yellow pepper – *chopped*

2 ribs celery – *chopped*

3 cloves garlic – minced OR 1 tsp. garlic powder

3 cups vegetable OR chicken broth

2 cups canned black beans

2 tsp. Cajun seasoning

¼ tsp. hot red pepper sauce

One 10 oz. pkg. frozen sliced okra

OPTIONAL: 8 oz. cooked diced pork, cooked diced chicken, peeled deveined shrimp

DIRECTIONS:

1. Cook rice according to package directions. OR use the 90-second rice.
2. **In large saucepan** over MEDIUM HEAT, cook oil and flour, stirring until golden brown—about 2 minutes.
3. Add peppers, celery, onion, and garlic. Cook about 8 minutes or till browned.
4. Slowly **whisk** in broth.
5. Add beans, and pork or chicken if used, Cajun seasoning, and pepper sauce. Bring to a BOIL. Reduce heat to LOW and simmer about 10 minutes till gumbo is thickened.
6. Add okra and shrimp if using. Return to boil; reduce heat to low and simmer about 5 minutes or till shrimp turns pink.
7. If desired, add ½ tsp. of Gumbo Filé to thicken. Serve over rice.

WHAT WE LEARNED:

✓ Add okra at the end of a recipe. If you overcook it, it will get slimy.

✓ Cook shrimp for only about 4-5 minutes or till it turns pink.

✓ Gumbo Filé is just sassafras. It will thicken a soup and make it a little cloudy. There's nothing wrong with that—it's just how it looks.

BUTTERNUT SQUASH SOUP - Stovetop

★ RIDICULOUSLY EASY

INGREDIENTS:

1 package frozen butternut squash

One 10-1/2 oz. can of chicken broth (= 1-1/4 cups)

8 oz. jar applesauce

DIRECTIONS:

1. In **medium-sized saucepan**, cook squash in broth till hot.
2. **Whisk** in applesauce.
3. Add salt & pepper if desired. Serve with a dollop of plain yogurt.

★

SWEET POTATO SOUP – Stovetop, blender/food processor

★ MODERATELY EASY

INGREDIENTS:

2 tsp. olive oil

1 small onion – *finely chopped*

1 tsp. ground cumin

1 sweet potato – *peeled and diced*

2 cups chicken broth

Salt and pepper

½ cup plain yogurt

3 tsp. chopped chives for garnish

DIRECTIONS:

1. Scrub sweet potato with vegetable brush. Peel with vegetable peeler. Dice.
2. In **heavy-bottomed stockpot**, over MEDIUM heat, heat olive oil for 60 seconds.
3. Add onion and cumin and sauté for 5 minutes, stirring frequently.
4. Add the sweet potato and chicken broth. Turn heat to HIGH and bring to a boil. Reduce heat and SIMMER until sweet potato is tender, 25 to 30 minutes.
5. Remove pot from heat and cool slightly, about 10 minutes.
6. Transfer soup to **food processor or blender** and blend at LOW SPEED. Don't fill the blender more than halfway or it may make a mess. If using immersion blender, you can just stick in pan and use without having to transfer the soup.
7. Return soup to pot and reheat it. Season with salt & pepper. Whisk in yogurt and serve with a sprinkling of chives.

WHAT WE LEARNED:

✓ You can just scrub and peel sweet potatoes, as opposed to boiling them and taking off the peel by hand.

✓ You shouldn't fill a blender more than halfway—unless you like cleaning up the kitchen, counters, and everything in its path.

✓ When using a blender, always make sure the top is secure AND KEEP YOUR HAND ON THE TOP WHILE IT'S BLENDING. I don't care how expensive your blender was, just do this. Some day you'll thank me.

✓ You cool soup for a bit, as you don't want to put boiling soup in a blender.

MORROCAN LAMB STEW – Stovetop, Crockpot – YIELD: 8

★ ADVANCED

If you love Mediterranean or North African food, you'll love this spiced stew.

INGREDIENTS:

3 lbs. lamb – *cut for stew meat into 1-1/2 inch pieces*

2-1/4 tsp. kosher salt

1-3/4 cups chicken stock

5 oz. (1 cup) dried apricots

2 T. olive oil

2 large onions – *chopped*

1 tsp. tomato paste

Large pinch saffron

½ tsp. ground ginger

¾ tsp. ground turmeric

¾ tsp. ground black pepper

¼ tsp. ground cinnamon

Pinch nutmeg

GARNISH:

2 scallions – *cut with scissors*

2 T. fresh parsley – *chopped*

Fresh lemon – *cut into serving wedges*

DIRECTIONS:

1. **In large bowl**, combine lamb and 2 tsp. salt. Let sit at room temperature for 1 hour or up to 24 hours in the refrigerator.
2. **In small saucepan**, bring stock to a boil. Remove from heat, add apricots, let sit for at least 15 minutes.
3. **In large skillet**, heat 2 T. oil over MEDIUM HEAT for 60 seconds. Working in batches, put lamb pieces in pot and cook till brown, about 10 minutes. Transfer finished lamb to a plate.
4. Add onions and ¼ tsp. salt to large skillet and cook till soft, about 5-8 minutes.
5. Add tomato paste and other spices and cook about 2 minutes.
6. Pour all the ingredients (except garnish) into a **crockpot** and cook on LOW for 8-10 hours.
7. Garnish and serve with a lemon wedge on each plate. Serve with couscous, flatbread, or rice.

★

NANCY'S VEGETABLE MINESTRONE SOUP - Stovetop

★ **EASY**

INGREDIENTS:

2 T. olive oil

2 medium zucchini – *cut in bite-sized pieces*

½ cup onion - *chopped*

2 cloves garlic – *minced* OR 1 tsp. garlic powder

1 tsp. Italian seasoning

½ tsp. salt

4 cups vegetable broth

¼ cup grated Parmesan cheese

1 can diced tomatoes

1 can cannellini beans – *rinsed*

2/3 cup elbow pasta - *cooked*

DIRECTIONS:

1. Cook pasta according to package directions. Set aside.
2. **In 6-quart pot**, heat olive oil on MEDIUM-HIGH HEAT.
3. Add zucchini, onion, Italian seasoning, and salt. Sauté 3-5 minutes.
4. Add broth and diced tomatoes.
5. COVER and SIMMER ON LOW 10 minutes.
6. Add garlic powder, cooked pasta, and beans to soup and SIMMER till heated through. Add Parmesan last.

MISCELLANEOUS

QUICHE – Preheat oven to 375°F, Serves 4-6

★ **EASY**

This is a fun recipe. You build it. There are a lot of variables, depending on your preferences. Use whatever meat you have, or none if you prefer. This is great for breakfast, brunch, lunch, supper, or a party.

INGREDIENTS:

Frozen pie crust

Pepper & onion (enough to cover bottom of pie crust) – *chopped*

½ cup of meat, chicken, or fish - *chopped*

1 cup cheese – *shredded* (whatever kind you like)

2 T. chive cream cheese

LIQUID PART:

½ cup mayonnaise (or ¾ cup if you like it rich)

2 eggs – *beaten*

¾ cup of milk (or evaporated milk or cream if you prefer)

Seasonings

DIRECTIONS:

1. Poke holes in **pie crust** in 4 places with a fork. Bake pie crust at 375°F for 10 minutes. Remove from oven and put in fillings.
2. In a **bowl with spout** combine the mayo, eggs, milk, and seasonings.
3. Pour over things in the pie crust.
4. Bake for 40 minutes or until butter knife inserted in center comes out clean.

WHAT WE LEARNED:

✓ Use your imagination with flavors. If you use shrimp, try seasoning the liquid part with dill or seafood seasoning. If you use leftover meatballs, season the liquid part with Italian seasoning—oregano and basil, for instance.

✓ How to use leftovers deliciously.

✓ Poking holes in pie crust allows steam to escape; keeps it from going convex.

★

DILL SOUFFLES – Preheat oven to 425°F. You'll need four 5-oz. soufflé dishes.

★ **EASY**

This recipe will make you feel like a real chef. Don't forget to buy buttermilk.

INGREDIENTS:

½ cup flour

½ cup buttermilk

2 eggs – *beaten*

1 egg white* – *beaten*

4 tsp. butter – *divided into 4 pats*

1 tsp. dried dill

8 tsp. grated Romano cheese

DIRECTIONS:

1. In a **bowl with spout**, beat 1st 4 ingredients until just combined.
2. Place 1 tsp. of butter in bottom of each of **four 5-oz. soufflé dishes.**
3. Place the dishes on a **cookie sheet.** Put in oven till butter melts, about 1 minute.
4. Take out of oven and sprinkle ¼ tsp. of dill in each dish.
5. Pour buttermilk mixture evenly into the 4 dishes.
6. Top each with 2 tsp. of Romano cheese.
7. Bake until golden brown and puffy, about 15 to 20 minutes.

WHAT WE LEARNED:

✓ That soufflés aren't just for experts!

✓ *How to separate an egg: crack the egg and hold upright. Switch back and forth, holding the shells together, letting the egg white drip out into a bowl. Don't let the yolk get pierced.

✓ Why you must use an actual soufflé dish – because the straight sides contain the soufflé as it rises.

★

GROWN-UP MAC 'N' CHEESE – Preheat oven to 400°F.

★ **MODERATELY EASY**

INGREDIENTS:

2 cups (8 oz) elbow macaroni

1 T. oil

¼ cup onion – *chopped fine*

3 cups milk, divided 2 + 1

1/3 cup flour

2 tsp. dry mustard OR prepared Dijon mustard

¾ tsp. salt

¼ tsp. white pepper (or black if you prefer)

½ tsp. paprika

½ tsp. ground rosemary

6 oz. cheddar cheese (3/4 cup)

3 T. breadcrumbs + 1 tsp. oil OR melted butter

DIRECTIONS:

1. Cook elbow macaroni according to package directions; drain.
2. In **large saucepan**, sauté onion in 1 T. oil till it starts to brown—about 6 minutes.
3. Add 2 cups of milk and heat till it shimmers (at or just below the boiling point)
4. In a **small bowl**, whisk the remaining cup of milk, the flour and spices, then add to saucepan. Cook just until it bubbles and thickens.
5. Now add the cheese, whisking until it melts.
6. Stir in the cooked macaroni, then put in a GREASED **2-quart baking dish**.
7. In a **small bowl**, mix breadcrumbs with 1 tsp. oil OR melted butter.
8. Sprinkle buttered breadcrumbs over macaroni and sprinkle with paprika.
9. Bake 10 minutes. Serves 6.

WHAT WE LEARNED:

✓ Definition of shimmer (at or below boiling point). It looks like it's moving.

★

<u>BAKED BEANS</u> –Preheat oven to 350°F OR use crockpot on LOW

★ **EASY**

INGREDIENTS:

Two 28 oz. cans baked beans

½ cup molasses

¾ cup onions – *chopped*

½ cup brown sugar

2 T. prepared mustard

½ cup ketchup

4 slices bacon – *chopped*

DIRECTIONS:

1. Drain beans.
2. In **large mixing bowl**, mix beans with molasses, onions, brown sugar, and ketchup.
3. Put in GREASED **casserole**. Top with chopped bacon if desired.
4. *If regular oven*: Bake at 350°F one hour until bubbly.
5. *If Crockpot:* Pour from bowl into crockpot and cook on LOW for 3 hours.

WHAT WE LEARNED:

✓ This is a great dish for a party. Heat and serve in the crockpot.

<u>PEANUTTY CHICKEN PASTA</u> – Stovetop recipe + microwave. Serves 2

★ EASY

This recipe has 3 sections: the pasta, the sauce, and the veggies. Then you put them all together for a heavenly dish. No measurements on chicken or veggies—use what you like. If you have more people, cook more pasta.

INGREDIENTS:

Angel Hair or Vermicelli pasta – for 2

Chicken – cooked, diced

Veggies – pepper, onion, mushrooms, zucchini, summer squash

Peanut oil

SAUCE:

¼ cup peanut butter

¼ cup mayo

¼ cup soy sauce

1 T. brown sugar

2 T. lemon juice

DIRECTIONS:

1. Cook pasta according to package directions. Drain well.
2. In a **large bowl**, whisk sauce ingredients together. It will look lumpy and weird, but ignore that.
3. In a **large frying pan**, sauté veggies in peanut oil till soft.
4. Add the cooked pasta and veggies to the large bowl of sauce and mix well. The sauce is not heated but adding the other ingredients to it will make it hot enough. If you prefer it hotter, pop it in the microwave for 2 minutes.

WHAT WE LEARNED:

✓ Peanut oil will give a nice Asian flavor to the food.

✓ Ingredients can look strange but come out great in the end.

✓ This recipe can easily be vegetarian—just leave out the chicken.

★

<u>PIZZA</u> – Preheat oven to 375°F.

★ EASY

INGREDIENTS:

Pizza crust – *pre-made*

2 cups shredded cheese – *divided*

¼ cup Parmesan cheese – *grated*

2 T. fresh basil OR 2 tsp. dried

2/3 cup mayonnaise

4 plum tomatoes – *sliced*

DIRECTIONS:

1. Put crust on **cookie sheet**. Sprinkle with 1 cup of cheese; set aside.
2. In **1-quart bowl**, combining remaining cup of cheese, parmesan, basil, and mayo. Mix well.
3. Thinly slice tomatoes; arrange in single layer over cheese on crust.
4. Using **small ice cream scoop**, place cheese/mayo mixture over tomatoes. Spread to cover evenly.
5. Bake 15-20 minutes or until top is golden brown and bubbly.

WHAT WE LEARNED:

✓ If you don't have a pizza crust handy or don't want to make one, you can always try putting this on pita bread.

CAJUN RED BEANS & RICE – Stovetop. Serves 5

★ **MODERATELY EASY**

INGREDIENTS:

4 cups cooked rice (= 2 cups *un*cooked rice)

2 T. olive oil

(2) 3 oz. andouille sausage links – *chopped*

8 oz. container of chopped onion, pepper, & celery – *or chop your own to = 1 cup*

1-1/2 tsp. Cajun seasoning

¾ tsp. salt

½ tsp. dried oregano

Garlic powder to taste

15 oz. can red kidney beans – *rinsed & drained*

¼ cup water

14.5 oz. can diced tomatoes OR about 3 fresh tomatoes – *diced*

¼ tsp. pepper

DIRECTIONS:

1. Cook rice first, according to package directions.
2. Heat olive oil in **large non-stick skillet** over MEDIUM HEAT. Add sausage and onion mix to pan. Sauté for 4 minutes.
3. Add Cajun seasoning, salt, oregano, garlic powder to pan. Cook 1 minute, stirring constantly.
4. In a **small bowl**, partially mash kidney beans with fork. Add beans, the ¼ cup of water, and tomatoes to skillet.
5. Bring to a boil (bubbles should just break the surface). Reduce heat; simmer 10 minutes or until thickened.
6. Remove from heat, stir in pepper. Serve over hot rice in a **shallow soup bowl**.

NOTE:

✓ If you want an authentic Cajun dish, try adding about 1/2 tsp. of Gumbo Filé to the dish. It will look a bit cloudy, like real Cajun dishes, and will get thicker. What is Gumbo Filé? It's actually just sassafras.

★

JAMBALAYA – Stovetop. Serves 4

★ **MODERATELY EASY**

INGREDIENTS:

2 T. butter

½ cup each of pepper & onion – *chopped*

1 cup rice – *uncooked*

2 cups broth – any flavor

1 can stewed tomatoes

1 tsp. Cajun seasoning

Garlic powder

Salt & pepper – I like Tony Chachere's, a spicy seasoning. Go hot if you like.

Andouille sausage – *chopped*

Ham – *diced*

Chicken – *cooked & diced*

Shrimp – *RAW, peeled and deveined* (usually can buy this way)

DIRECTIONS:

1. In **large skillet**, melt butter. Sauté pepper and onion about 5 minutes.
2. Add UNCOOKED rice and sauté for 1 minute, deglazing the pan.
3. Add stock. Bring to a boil.
4. Add tomatoes and seasonings.
5. COVER and cook on LOW heat till rice is cooked, about 20 minutes. Taste it to make sure rice is cooked properly.
6. Once rice is how you like it, add the sausage, ham, chicken, shrimp—whatever you like. If using raw shrimp, cook until shrimp no longer turns pink, NO MORE THAN ABOUT 6-8 MINUTES.

WHAT WE LEARNED:

✓ Deglazing the pan means removing/dissolving browned food residue from the pan, thereby not wasting any "goodness" as my mom used to say.

✓ How uncooked rice gets cooked in a recipe like this.

✓ How to determine doneness of shrimp. A recipe I tried once called for it to cook for 45 minutes! When you learn to cook, you also learn when someone has given you the wrong directions.

✓ How to try different flavors—chicken broth when making a chicken Jambalaya, clam broth when making a seafood one, etc.

<u>**HUMMUS**</u> – Blender recipe

★ **EASY**

INGREDIENTS:

2 cans chickpeas – *drained and rinsed*

2/3 cup sesame tahini

½ tsp. dried cumin

¼ tsp. garlic powder

¼ cup olive oil

DIRECTIONS:

1. Combine chickpeas, tahini, and cumin in a **blender**.
2. With blender on HIGH, slowly drizzle in through the hole in the cover the ¼ cup of olive oil. Blend till hummus is smooth and creamy.
3. If needed, thin hummus with water to reach desired consistency.
4. Add salt and garlic powder to taste.
5. Serve with crackers, pita bread, or baby carrots.

NOTE:

Homemade hummus keeps in the refrigerator for only about 5 days. Put a strip of tape on the container with the date you made it.

BLT

★ EASY

The quality of the bread, bacon, and tomatoes (hopefully fresh and red) makes a big difference in this sandwich.

INGREDIENTS:

White bread

Cooked bacon – of *good quality*

Tomatoes – *sliced*

Lettuce

Mayonnaise

Salt & pepper

DIRECTIONS:

1. Toast bread if desired.
2. Slather mayonnaise liberally on both sides of bread.
3. Lay on the bacon (about 2 strips per sandwich)
4. Lay on the sliced tomatoes to cover. Put salt & pepper on tomatoes.
5. Lay on the lettuce last.

★

PERFECT GRILLED CHEESE SANDWICH – stovetop - griddle pan

★ EASY

I have, unfortunately, seen badly made grilled cheese sandwiches. Following my recipe for the Perfect Grilled Cheese Sandwich will ensure that it never happens to you.

INGREDIENTS:

2 pieces of bread – your choice

1 slice of cheese – I like cheddar, but American is good also

Butter for bread

Chive cream cheese

(optional) Tomato – *sliced*

(optional) 1 slice of ham or bacon

———————

DIRECTIONS:

1. Butter both sides of bread. Lay on **griddle**, butter side down.
2. Slather chive cream cheese on the unbuttered sides of bread.
3. Lay sliced cheese on cream cheese side.
4. Put tomato and/or ham/bacon if used.
5. Put other piece of bread on top, butter side up.
6. Cook till golden brown, then carefully flip to other side. When you flip to second side, use a hamburger press (if you have one) to weigh it down. This will make it cook faster and result in a crispy sandwich.

WHAT WE LEARNED:

✓ That a perfect grilled cheese should be made with quality ingredients, be flavorful, melty on the inside, and crispy on the outside.

✓ This perfect comfort food goes well with cream of tomato soup.

✓ Don't be afraid to experiment with different ingredients, maybe pineapple cream cheese if you're using ham, etc.

★

PACKET POTATOES – grill preheated to med-high OR oven, preheated to 450°F

★ **EASY**

INGREDIENTS:

Heavy duty aluminum foil, 18" x 24"

1 small onion – *thinly sliced*

4 medium potatoes – *cut in bite sized pieces*

2 T. olive oil or vegetable oil

1 tsp. seasoned salt

½ tsp. dried dill weed

¼ tsp. pepper

¼ tsp. ground thyme

———————————

DIRECTIONS:

1. Spray **foil** with nonstick spray.
2. Center onion on sheet of foil. Layer potatoes evenly on top of onion.
3. Drizzle with oil.
4. Sprinkle with seasonings.
5. Bring up sides of foil and double fold ends to closed and form one large foil packet, leaving room for heat circulation inside packet.

Oven: Bake 30-35 minutes on a cookie sheet.

Grill: Cook 15 to 20 minutes in COVERED grill.

WHAT WE LEARNED:

✓ How to make an easy recipe ahead of time if you're having a cookout. This leaves you time to visit with your guests.

★

PACKET VEGGIES– grill preheated to med-high OR oven, preheated to 450°F

★ **EASY**

INGREDIENTS:

Heavy duty aluminum foil, 18" x 18"

8 oz. whole fresh mushrooms

8 oz. cherry tomatoes

1 cup zucchini - *sliced*

1 T. olive oil

1 T. butter – *melted*

1/2 tsp. salt

½ tsp. onion powder

½ tsp. Italian seasoning

1/8 tsp. garlic powder

¼ tsp. pepper

DIRECTIONS:

1. Spray **foil** with nonstick spray.
2. Place vegetables on foil.
3. Combine butter, oil, and seasonings and drizzle over veggies.
4. Bring up sides of foil and double fold ends to closed and form one large foil packet, leaving room for heat circulation inside packet.

Oven: Bake 35-40 minutes on a cookie sheet.

Grill: Cook 20 to 25 minutes in COVERED grill.

WHAT WE LEARNED:

✓ How to make an easy recipe ahead of time if you're having a cookout. This leaves you time to visit with your guests.

★

DESReturnSERTS

DESSERTS

VINNIE'S RASPBERRY TARTLETS – Preheat oven to 450°F

★ MODERATELY EASY

My mother used to make these when she had a Tupperware party or a Ladies Postal Auxiliary meeting coming up. Sometimes she'd even let us have some!

INGREDIENTS:

Ready-made pie crust from the dairy case

Flour (to keep dough from sticking to surface)

1 jar of raspberry jam

1 egg, mixed with 1 T. water - *beaten*

Confectioner's sugar for dusting after baking

DIRECTIONS:

1. Spray **cookie sheet** with cooking spray.

1. Remove pie crusts from pouches; unroll on floured work surface.
2. Using a knife, cut out squares about 3" x 3"
3. Place squares on cookie sheet.
4. Place 1-2 teaspoons of jam in center of each dough piece.
5. Fold up 4 sides into a pouch or 2 sides for a diamond shape.
6. Press lightly on top.
7. Cut 2 small slits in top crust. Brush tops with egg/water mixture
8. Bake 10 to 13 minutes or until light golden brown.
9. Remove from cookie sheet to **cooling rack**; cool completely.
10. Sprinkle confectioner's sugar over all.

WHAT WE LEARNED:

✓ Use an egg wash on pastry crust to give it a more attractive, glossy finish.

✓ Sprinkle confectioner's sugar on COOLED crust. Otherwise, the confectioner's sugar will just melt. You want it to look powdery.

CATHEDRAL CANDY

★ EASY

INGREDIENTS:

1 stick butter

6 oz. package chocolate chips

½ bag colored mini-marshmallows

1 cup nuts – *chopped*

DIRECTIONS:

1. In a **medium-sized mixing bowl**, melt butter with chocolate chips in microwave, 30 seconds at a time till all is melted. Don't overcook or chocolate will be ruined!
2. Stir in marshmallows and nuts. Mix well.
3. Lay mixture on wax paper.
4. Roll up into a log and fold in ends.
5. Refrigerate.
6. When it's cold and solid, it's ready to slice.

WHAT WE LEARNED:

✓ That chocolate must never, ever be overcooked.

★

FRANK'S APPLE BROWN BETTY - Preheat oven to 350°F

★ **EASY**

INGREDIENTS:

1 cup + 2 T. brown sugar

½ cup homemade bread crumbs (see What We Learned, below)

1 stick unsalted butter – *room temperature*

8 Pippin, Greening, or McIntosh apples – *peeled, cored, thinly sliced*

Cinnamon

———————————

DIRECTIONS:

1. Butter a **1-1/2 quart baking dish or casserole**
2. Combine first 3 ingredients in **small bowl** and mix well.
3. Layer 1/3 of the apples in dish.
4. Cover with 1/3 of the crumbs. Sprinkle with cinnamon.
5. Repeat till dish is filled, ENDING WITH CRUMBS.
6. Cover with foil; bake 30 minutes (convection oven).
7. Remove foil. Bake another 20 minutes or till browned.
8. Serve warm with vanilla ice cream or whipped cream.

WHAT WE LEARNED:

✓ That apple desserts are a bit of work, but they're worth it.

✓ To make homemade bread crumbs, use dry, stale bread and just crumble with hands or put in food processor. Do not use fresh bread.

✓ I find peeling the apple while it's whole is easier than cutting, then peeling.

NAKED APPLE PIE – Preheat oven to 350°F

★ **EASY**

I have been shown how to make pie crusts since I began cooking at age 12. I've had old hands show me, cooking teachers show me, and seen numerous lessons on TV cooking shows. My crusts still look like a 5-year old made them. No problem. This recipe has no crust.

INGREDIENTS:

1 egg – *beaten*

½ cup brown sugar

½ cup white sugar

1 tsp. vanilla

Pinch salt

½ cup flour

1 tsp. baking powder

2 medium apples – *peeled, cored, and sliced*

½ cup nuts

DIRECTIONS:

1. In a **medium-sized mixing bowl**, blend all ingredients together.
2. Put into a GREASED **9" pie plate**.
3. Bake 30 minutes at 350°F.
4. Serve with vanilla ice cream.

★

CHOCOLATE BANANA PUDDING PIE – no bake

★ EASY

I don't know a soul in the world who doesn't like the combo of bananas and chocolate. This recipe can be made lower calorie by using sugar-free pudding.

INGREDIENTS:

4 oz. Baker's® semi-sweet chocolate (the whole package)

2 T. milk

1 T. butter

1 prepared graham cracker crust OR make your own (regular crust works, too)

2 medium bananas

2-3/4 cups cold milk

2 packages (4-serving size) vanilla OR banana cream INSTANT pudding

1-1/2 cups Cool Whip® – *THAWED*

DIRECTIONS:

1. In a **small bowl**, mix chocolate, milk, and butter and microwave on HIGH 1 to 1-1/2 minutes, stirring every 30 seconds. Chocolate should be completely melted.
2. Spread chocolate evenly in **crust**.
3. Refrigerate 30 minutes or till chocolate is firm.
4. Slice bananas and lay over chocolate.
5. In **large mixing bowl**, pour 2-3/4 cups of milk and add pudding mixes.
6. Beat with wire whisk one minute. Let stand 5 minutes to thicken.
7. Spoon pudding over bananas in crust. Spread with whipped topping.

WHAT WE LEARNED:

✓ Bananas should be sliced at the last minute or they turn brown.

✓ To make your own graham cracker crust, crush 10 full-sheet graham crackers, add 1/3 cup white sugar, 6 T. melted butter and mix together. If you like a firmer crust, bake at 325°F for 7 minutes and let cool before adding filling.

✓ If you are a chocolate addict like myself, try doubling the amount of chocolate. Can you really have too much chocolate?

★

10-MINUTE GERMAN SWEET CHOCOLATE CREAM PIE – no bake

★ EASY

INGREDIENTS:

1 package (4 oz.) Baker's® German's Sweet chocolate (the whole package)

1/3 cup milk

2 T. white sugar

3 oz. cream cheese (about half a package) – *softened*

3-1/2 cups (8 oz. container) Cool Whip® – *THAWED*

8-inch graham cracker crumb crust

DIRECTIONS:

1. In **small saucepan**, heat chocolate and 2 T. of the milk over LOW HEAT, stirring until chocolate is melted. DON'T WALK AWAY.
2. In **large mixing bowl**, beat sugar into cream cheese, using a **mixer**.
3. Add remaining milk and chocolate mixture and beat till smooth.
4. By hand, fold in whipped topping with a **spatula**, blending till smooth.
5. Pour into **crust**.
6. Freeze till firm, about 4 hours. Garnish with chocolate curls if desired.
7. Store any leftover pie (if there is any) in freezer.

WHAT WE LEARNED:

✓ I say DON'T WALK AWAY because your beautiful chocolate will burn if you leave it unattended.

✓ Chocolate curls can be done using a vegetable peeler. A lemon zester can also be used on firm chocolate, but the result will be smaller pieces.

✓ You fold in the Cool Whip® by hand because doing it gently won't deflate the nice puffy air of the ingredients. Folding is done slowly and using a certain technique where you scrape the bottom of the bowl to combine the two mixtures—no aggressive stirring! Cut straight down the center with a wide, flexible spatula all the way to the bottom of the bowl. Scrape along the bottom of the bowl towards you, continue up the side and scoop the mixture over the top. Continue till all ingredients are incorporated.

ROSE'S RICOTTA PIE – Preheat oven to 350°F

★ RIDICULOUSLY EASY

If you need something nice to bribe the admissions lady at Columbia with so you can get your little daughter Meadow admitted, this is just the thing. Rose was from Italy and this is the real deal. It tastes like the inside of a cannoli.

INGREDIENTS:

1-1/2 lbs. ricotta cheese

3 eggs – *beaten*

2 tsp. orange juice

2 tsp. lemon juice

¾ cup sugar

Pie crust

DIRECTIONS:

1. In **large mixing bowl,** dump in all ingredients and mix well with a wire whisk.
2. Pour into a pie crust like one of those found in the dairy case. You just let it sit at room temperature for 15 minutes, then unfold and put into a **deep pie plate**. Crimp the edges and pour in the filling. Put a skinny piece of aluminum foil around the edges to keep them from overbrowning.
3. Bake at 350°F for 60 minutes or till knife inserted into center comes out clean. Keep refrigerated.

WHAT WE LEARNED:

✓ How easy a classic recipe can be.

✓ Try mini-chocolate chips in the batter before baking.

★

DEBORAH LOU'S ECLAIR RING – Preheat oven to 400°F

★ ADVANCED

This recipe feels weird as you're preparing it (building it, really). But when you're done, you have a professional-looking product and you'll feel like a pastry chef.

SHELL INGREDIENTS:

1 stick butter

1 cup water

1 cup flour

4 eggs

FILLING INGREDIENTS:

2 boxes INSTANT vanilla pudding

1 pint whipping cream*

1 cup milk

1 tsp. vanilla extract

FROSTING:

1 container chocolate frosting

DIRECTIONS:

1. In **large saucepan**, heat butter and water to boiling.
2. Take off stove. Add flour.
3. Beat in eggs, one at a time. The batter will get shiny.
4. Blob on a **pizza pan** in the shape of a ring. Try using an **ice cream scoop**, then connect edges so it forms a complete ring.
5. Bake 30 minutes at 400°F. Turn off stove and leave in oven for 30 minutes. Don't open the oven door while it's resting!
6. Slice ring in half horizontally, like it's an English muffin. Scoop out the eggy parts with the **grapefruit spoon** I told you to buy and discard eggy parts.
7. In a **large mixing bowl**, mix filling with a whisk. Let harden 20 minutes.
8. Fill bottom half of ring with filling. Put on ring top. Now doesn't it look like an éclair?
9. Melt frosting and pour over all. Keep refrigerated.

Whipping cream is found in the dairy section, not to be confused with *whipped* cream.

★

<u>WATERGATE CAKE</u> – Preheat oven to 350°F

★ **EASY**

INGREDIENTS:

3 eggs

1 package of devil's food cake mix.

1 package INSTANT chocolate pudding

1 cup vegetable oil

<u>1 cup club soda</u>

Confectioner's sugar for garnish

OR icing

DIRECTIONS:

1. Thoroughly GREASE a **Bundt pan**.
2. In a **large mixing bowl**, mix all ingredients together. Use a **hand mixer** set on LOW speed to beat everything together for 30 seconds. Switch mixer to a MEDIUM-HIGH setting, and beat for an additional 1 to 2 minutes. This is going to make your cake light and fluffy.
3. Bake at 350°F for 45 minutes or till tester inserted in center comes out clean.
4. When it is done baking, take it out of the oven and cool on a **wire rack**. Make absolutely sure it is <u>completely</u> cool before you remove it. Use a knife or thin rubber spatula to loosen the cake from the sides of the pan before turning it over onto a plate.
5. Dust confectioner's sugar on completely cooled cake OR frost with either cream cheese icing or chocolate ganache.

WHAT WE LEARNED:

✓ This is called the Watergate cake because the original recipe was filled with nuts and covered in fluff, ostensibly like the Nixon administration had been.[8] The original recipe, promoted by the Jell-O® test kitchens, was made with pistachio pudding and white cake mix.

★

LOUISE'S CARROT CAKE – Preheat oven to 350°F

★ **EASY**

This recipe comes from the mother of one of my best friends, who made this cake for her husband when he went off hunting. It's got enough calories that, if you were lost in the woods of New Hampshire for a few days, it would keep you alive. That said, it's the absolute best carrot cake in the world.

INGREDIENTS:

3 cups carrots (4 carrots) – *shredded* –

easy if you have a food processor with the grating attachment

2 cups granulated white sugar

4 eggs

2 cups flour

½ cup nuts – *chopped*

2 tsp. baking soda

1 tsp. salt

2 tsp. ground cinnamon

DIRECTIONS:

1. In a **large mixing bowl**, combine oil and sugar.
2. Beat well, then beat in eggs, one at a time, while continuing to beat on HIGH speed.
3. Add flour, baking soda, salt, and cinnamon. Mix well.
4. Fold in shredded carrots and nuts.
5. Bake in GREASED **9" x 13" pan** at 350°F for 40 minutes.
6. Ice with cream cheese icing.

WHAT WE LEARNED:

✓ This is a great party cake. Cut into squares small enough to fit in cupcake liners for guests to grab and eat easily.

✓ Keep refrigerated because the icing has cream cheese in it.

CHRISTINA'S TRIFLE

★ **EASY**

This looks pretty for a party in its special trifle dish. If you're really in a hurry, just buy a pre-made cake and a pint of pudding in the dairy case and build this. Try this with different cake and pudding combos.

INGREDIENTS:

2 packages INSTANT chocolate pudding – *prepared as directed*

1 chocolate cake mix – *prepared as directed*

2 large tubs Cool Whip®

3 Skor® or Heath candy bars - *chopped*

DIRECTIONS:

1. Bake chocolate cake in a **sheet pan or 9" x 13" pan** as directed on package. When cooled, cut into bite-sized cubes.
2. In a **large mixing bowl**, prepare chocolate pudding as directed on package.
3. In a **glass trifle dish** (deep sides, often on a pedestal) layer the ingredients in several layers as follows:

- Cake cubes
- Pudding
- Cool Whip®
- Chopped candy bars
- End the layers with whipped cream on top, garnish with candy

VIENNESE ALMOND BARS – Preheat oven to 375°F

★ **MODERATELY EASY**

INGREDIENTS:

3 T. firm butter

1-1/2 cups Bisquick®

3 T. packed brown sugar

½ cup apricot preserves

1 can (8 oz.) almond paste – *room temperature*

2 T. Bisquick® baking mix

½ tsp. vanilla extract

2 eggs

1 package (6 oz. OR 1 cup) semi-sweet chocolate chips

DIRECTIONS:

1. In **medium-sized mixing bowl**, cut butter into 1-1/2 cups baking mix and brown sugar until mixture resembles fine crumbs. A pastry cutter is helpful.
2. Lightly press into UNGREASED **square pan, 9" x 9" x 2"**.
3. Bake at 375°F until edges are very light brown, 12-15 minutes.
4. Stir preserves to soften; carefully spread over <u>hot</u> baked layer.
5. In a **small mixing bowl** break almond paste into ½ inch pieces. Beat almond paste, 2 T. baking mix, vanilla, and eggs on LOW SPEED, scraping bowl constantly till smooth, about 2 minutes.
6. Spoon over preserves; spread slightly to cover.
7. Bake until golden brown, 20-22 minutes.
8. Remove from oven and sprinkle hot squares with chocolate chips; let stand until softened; about 5 minutes. Spread chocolate carefully; cool.
9. Cut into bars.

WHAT WE LEARNED:

 ✓ Almond paste can be found in the baking aisle.

★

PUFFY STUFF

★ EASY

INGREDIENTS:

16 oz. vanilla yogurt (2 cups)

1 package Jell-O® – any flavor

¼ cup BOILING water

8 oz. Cool Whip® (one container)

DIRECTIONS:

1. Dissolve Jell-O® in the ¼ cup of boiling water in a small measuring cup. Whisk for 2 minutes, making sure it's all dissolved.
2. Whisk dissolved Jell-O® into yogurt
3. Fold in Cool Whip® by hand with a spatula till it's all incorporated.
4. Let set for about 2 hours in refrigerator.
5. Serve with fruit on top if desired. Keep refrigerated.

OPTIONS:

Orange Jell-O® with mandarin oranges

Raspberry Jell-O® with fresh raspberries

Strawberry Jell-O® with fresh strawberry slices

WHAT WE LEARNED:

✓ If you don't dissolve the gelatin thoroughly, you'll get little chunks of it in the final product.

✓ I'd use the traditional Cool Whip® in this recipe. I tried a different type (what I thought was similar) and it didn't set right.

★

CHOCOLATE PUDDING - Stovetop

★ EASY

This is one of the first things I learned in Home Economics cooking class. It's fun to add things to it to make it your way.

INGREDIENTS:

2 T. sugar

2 T. unsweetened baking cocoa powder

2 T. cornstarch

2 cups lowfat milk

1 tsp. vanilla extract

1 T. butter

DIRECTIONS:

1. In a **medium-sized saucepan**, put sugar, cocoa, and cornstarch and make a paste with a little of the milk, whisking it together.
2. Slowly add the remaining milk.
3. Cook on LOW, whisking constantly, till thick—about 5 minutes.
4. Remove from heat. Add the vanilla and butter. Stir till melted.
5. Pour into a bowl; cover. Refrigerate for a few hours or till set.

Pop quiz question: what is it that makes the pudding thick?

Answer: the cornstarch.

TRY ONE OF THESE OPTIONS:

- Add 1 Tablespoon or two of peanut butter; mix thoroughly.
- ½ tsp. mint extract
- ½ tsp. almond extract
- Mini chocolate chips to finished product
- Caramel chips to finished product

★

<u>**INDIAN PUDDING**</u> – Stovetop and oven preheated to 350°F

★ **EASY**

This is a great old New England recipe reminiscent of Olde Sturbridge Village. The perfect thing for autumn.

INGREDIENTS:

2 eggs

¾ cup molasses

1/3 cup firmly packed dark brown sugar

1 tsp. ground cinnamon

1 tsp. ground ginger

½ tsp. salt

¼ tsp. baking soda

4 cups milk – *divided*

2/3 cup yellow cornmeal

3 T. unsalted butter

Vanilla ice cream for garnish

DIRECTIONS:

1. **Butter** a deep **1-1/2 quart baking dish**.
2. In a **large, deep saucepan**, combine eggs, molasses, sugar, spices, salt, baking soda and just 2-1/2 cups of the milk and whisk till blended.
3. **Whisk** in cornmeal.
4. Cook over MEDIUM HEAT, stirring constantly, till mixture bubbles and becomes stiff.
5. Remove from heat.
6. Add butter and remaining 1-1/2 cups of milk and stir till smooth. Don't worry, it will thicken upon baking.
7. Turn into baking dish and bake till pudding is still slightly soft in center, about 1-1/4 hours. Pudding will continue to firm as it cools.

★

BANANA BREAD PUDDING – Preheat oven to 375°F

★ **MODERATELY EASY**

PUDDING INGREDIENTS:

¼ cup (half a stick) butter

3 c. (3 slices) white bread – *cubed*

½ cup sugar

2 cups milk

1 large banana – *sliced*

3 eggs

½ tsp. cinnamon

½ tsp. nutmeg

¼ tsp. salt

2 tsp. vanilla extract

PUDDING DIRECTIONS:

1. In **2-quart casserole** melt butter in oven.
2. Add bread cubes. Stir to mix.
3. In **small mixing bowl**, combine remaining pudding ingredients. Mix well. Pour over bread cubes; stir to coat.
4. Bake 40 to 50 minutes or till knife inserted in center comes out clean.

SAUCE INGREDIENTS:

½ cup (1 stick) butter

2 cups confectioner's (powdered) sugar

¼ cup milk

¼ tsp. cinnamon

2 T. lemon juice

1 tsp. rum extract

SAUCE DIRECTIONS:

1. **In large saucepan**, melt 1 stick butter over LOW heat.
2. Combine remaining sauce ingredients; stir.

3. Cook over LOW heat, stirring constantly till it comes to a full boil—2 to 3 minutes.

4. To serve, pour 1/3 cup of sauce over each serving or serve on the side.

<u>VANILLA CUSTARD CUPS</u> – Preheat oven to 350°F. Serves 2

★ **EASY**

INGREDIENTS:

1 egg – *beaten*

1 cup milk

3 T. brown sugar

¾ tsp. vanilla extract

1/8 tsp. salt

1/8 tsp. ground nutmeg

DIRECTIONS:

1. In a **small mixing bowl**, beat the egg, then **whisk** in milk, brown sugar, vanilla, and salt. Mix till blended.
2. Pour into custard cups. Will *almost* fill **<u>four</u> 4 oz. custard cups**.
3. Sprinkle with nutmeg.
4. Put a dish towel in the bottom of a **9-inch square baking pan**. Place cups in pan. Fill pan with HOT water to a depth of 1 inch.
5. Bake UNCOVERED at 350°F for 25 minutes or till a butter knife inserted in the center comes out clean.

WHAT WE LEARNED:

✓ The method of placing cups in a towel-lined pan and adding water is called a bain-marie or, in English, a water bath. *A water bath insulates custards from the direct heat of the oven because the water can't exceed 212°F, unlike the air in a 350°F oven. Without a water bath, the outside of your dessert would overcook before the center is done. And direct heat could take small custards, like pudding cakes, from cooked to cracked within a minute.*[9]

MAPLE-PUMPKIN CUSTARDS – Preheat oven to 325°F. Serves 6

★ **MODERATELY EASY**

INGREDIENTS:

4 large eggs – *beaten*

1-1/2 cups 1% milk

¾ cup maple syrup (Grade B Dark Amber if possible)

¾ cup canned unseasoned pumpkin puree

1 tsp. ground cinnamon

½ tsp. ground nutmeg

¼ tsp. salt

Whipped cream & crystallized ginger

DIRECTIONS:

1. Boil 4-6 cups water for a water bath. Line a **9" x 13" roasting pan** with a folded kitchen towel.
2. In a **small saucepan**, heat milk over low heat till barely steaming but not boiling.
3. In a **large mixing bowl**, whisk eggs and maple syrup till smooth.
4. Gently whisk in warm milk, a little at a time, so the eggs don't cook.
5. Add pumpkin, cinnamon, nutmeg, and salt. Whisk till blended.
6. Divide mixture among **six 6 oz. custard cups**. Put in towel-lined pan. Pour boiling water into pan till it comes halfway up sides of custard cups.
7. Bake UNCOVERED at 325°F for 45 minutes (in convection oven) or till custards are just set but still quiver in center when shaken.
8. Transfer to wire rack; cool 45 minutes. Cover and refrigerate at least one hour. Serve with whipped cream and a sprinkling of crystallized ginger.

WHAT WE LEARNED:

✓ The method of placing cups in a towel-lined pan and adding water is called a bain-marie or, in English, a water bath. *A water bath insulates custards from the direct heat of the oven because the water can't exceed 212°F, unlike the air in a 350°F oven. Without a water bath, the outside of your dessert would overcook before the center is done. And direct heat could take small custards, like pudding cakes, from cooked to cracked within a minute.*[10]

★

HOT WATER GINGERBREAD – Preheat oven to 375°F

★ EASY

INGREDIENTS:

½ cup molasses

½ cup boiling water

½ cup brown sugar }

1-1/2 cups flour } dry ingredients

1 tsp. baking powder }

1 tsp. baking soda }

1 tsp. ground ginger }

¼ tsp. salt }

4 T. butter – *melted*

——————————

DIRECTIONS:

1. In the **measuring cup** in which you boiled the half cup of water in the microwave, add the molasses. Mix well.
2. In a **large mixing bowl**, mix all the dry ingredients.
3. Add the melted butter last and beat well by hand. Taste it. Add more cinnamon and nutmeg if you like it spicier.
4. GREASE a **square brownie pan**. Pour in batter and bake for 30 minutes or till tester or toothpick inserted in center comes out clean. Serve with whipped cream OR my Tangy Lemon Dessert Sauce.

WHAT WE LEARNED:

✓ Molasses was used in America prior to the 20th century as a sweetener. It has more vitamins and minerals than white refined sugar.

✓ A word about brown sugar. Some recipes specify light or dark brown sugar. Dark brown sugar has twice as much molasses in it and has a stronger flavor. It is probably a matter of taste. Also, if dark brown sugar will make the recipe look too dark, use the light brown sugar instead.

✓ When measuring brown sugar, always pack it tightly into the measuring cup.

★

LEMON PUDDING CAKE – Preheat oven to 350°F

★ **EASY**

This recipe is in 3 layers. It's easy to serve for a party, as you can cut in squares.

INGREDIENTS:

1 cup flour

½ cup butter (1 stick) – *room temperature*

1/3 cup walnuts – *finely crushed*

1 cup confectioner's sugar

8 oz. package of cream cheese – *room temperature*

12 oz. container of Cool Whip® - *divided*

2 pkgs. Lemon INSTANT pudding

Milk to make pudding

DIRECTIONS:

1. In **medium sized mixing bowl**, mix flour, butter, and nuts. Press into **9" x 13" pan**. Bake for 12 to 15 minutes or till light golden brown. Cool in refrigerator.
2. In **large mixing bowl**, mix confectioner's sugar, cream cheese, and 1 cup of the Cool Whip®. Spread on cooled crust. Try using an ice cream scoop, then connect to cover crust.
3. In **medium mixing bowl**, mix pudding with milk as directed on package. Let stand 5 minutes. Put pudding on top of mixture in pan. Cool 1 hour.
4. Put remaining whipped topping on top. Keep refrigerated.

WHAT WE LEARNED:

✓ How to "build" a layered dessert.

★

MICROWAVE-BAKED APPLES - Microwave

★ EASY

INGREDIENTS:

2 apples (Gala is good) – *cored, halved, peeled*

2 tsp. butter

2 tsp. water

½ tsp. sugar

1/8 tsp. ground cinnamon

2 T. raisins

4 T. yogurt for garnish – maple or vanilla

DIRECTIONS:

1. Place apples, cut sides up, in **9-inch glass pie plate or casserole**.
2. Dot with butter
3. Sprinkle evenly with water, sugar, and cinnamon.
4. Cover dish with wax paper and microwave on HIGH till apples are very tender, about 5 minutes.
5. Add raisins and let stand, covered, 2 minutes.
6. Serve with yogurt either on top or as a base for the apples.

WHAT WE LEARNED:

✓ How quickly you can make a healthy dessert.

✓ Raisins should be added at the end. If you cook them with the apples, they'll get hard. It's a different story if they're going into a batter.

POACHED PEARS - Stovetop

★ EASY

Pairing chocolate with things you might not expect is very European. My dad, whose parents came from Sicily, used to make us Sunday breakfast, which was Italian bread, torn into chunks and put in a bowl, with hot chocolate poured over it. The combo of sweet and the slightly salty bread was great. My Dutch mother-in-law used to have shaved chocolate on bread and butter. Expand your palate!

INGREDIENTS:

2 cups sweet wine – I like white zinfandel

½ cup sugar

2 T. lemon juice

4 Bosc pears – *peeled, cored, and halved*

Vanilla ice cream for garnish

Chocolate sauce for garnish

DIRECTIONS:

1. Boil water in a **medium-sized saucepan**. Dip pears in for 30 seconds. Put in a bowl of warm water. Peels should come off easily with vegetable peeler. Core with grapefruit knife or apple peeler. Or just cut away the core.
2. In a **small heavy saucepan** bring wine and sugar to a boil. Lower heat and simmer for 5 more minutes.
3. Add lemon juice and pears. Cook for 10 minutes over MEDIUM HEAT. Cool and refrigerate.
4. Bring the pears to room temperature before serving. Serve with either vanilla ice cream on top or a pool of melted dark chocolate under the pears.
5. TO MAKE CHOCOLATE SAUCE: Put dark chocolate or chocolate chips in a glass measuring cup. Barely cover with milk. Melt in microwave till melted, about 30 seconds at 50%. Do not overcook!

WHAT WE LEARNED:

✓ How to make it easier to peel fruit. This works for tomatoes, too.

✓ Why lemon juice? Adding lemon juice keeps the fruit from turning brown.

DESSERT SAUCES AND FROSTINGS

PEANUT BUTTER FROSTING – electric stand mixer or hand mixer

★ RIDICULOUSLY EASY

INGREDIENTS:

1 T. butter – *softened*

¼ cup organic peanut butter

1-1/2 cups confectioner's sugar

½ tsp. vanilla

2 T. milk

DIRECTIONS:

In electric mixer bowl or **deep mixing bowl**, combine all and beat with electric mixer till smooth.

NOTE: Put on *Kid Again Brownies*, *Watergate Cake*—the possibilities are endless.

WHAT WE LEARNED:

✓ Why a deep mixing bowl? Because mixing frosting in an electric mixer causes it to fly all over the place, including on you. The high sides keep it in the bowl.

<u>CREAM CHEESE ICING</u> – electric stand mixer or hand mixer

★ RIDICULOUSLY EASY

INGREDIENTS:

One 8 oz. package cream cheese - *room temperature*

Half a stick of butter – *room temperature*

1 box (16 oz. or 1 lb.) confectioner's sugar

2 tsp. vanilla extract

———————

DIRECTIONS:

In electric mixer bowl or **deep mixing bowl**, combine all and beat with electric mixer till smooth.

———————

WHAT WE LEARNED:

✓ Why a deep mixing bowl? Because mixing frosting in an electric mixer causes it to fly all over the place, including on you. The high sides keep it in the bowl.

✓ If you put cream cheese icing on something, it's okay to leave out for the party or the day, but put away overnight in the refrigerator.

———————

NOTES: DELICIOUS ON carrot cake (see Desserts chapter) or chocolate cake.

★

CHOCOLATE GANACHE – Stovetop

★ RIDICULOUSLY EASY

Even though this is an adaptation of a Martha Stewart recipe (who makes her own English muffins for some reason), this is so easy and elegant.

INGREDIENTS:

½ cup heavy cream

3-1/2 ounces dark chocolate, 70% cacao preferably – *finely chopped*

1 T. unsalted butter – *softened*

———————————

DIRECTIONS:

1. In a **small saucepan**, bring cream <u>just</u> to a boil over MEDIUM-HIGH HEAT. Remove from heat.
2. In a **medium-sized HEATPROOF BOWL** put chopped chocolate.
3. Pour boiled cream over chocolate. Let stand for 2 minutes.
4. Add butter, then **whisk** mixture until smooth. If you want it to stay shiny, frost cake immediately.

WHAT WE LEARNED:

✓ When they say "just to a boil" take that literally. Once you see it boil, remove from heat or it may boil over.

✓ This will keep at room temperature for two days or two weeks in the refrigerator.

✓ **Variations:** Add ½ tsp. espresso powder, or 1 tsp. vanilla extract, or 1 tsp. almond extract . . . be creative.

★

TANGY LEMON DESSERT SAUCE - Stovetop

★ EASY

INGREDIENTS:

½ cup unsalted butter

1 cup white granulated sugar

3 T. water

2 T. lemon juice

1 T. grated lemon peel

2 eggs – *beaten*

DIRECTIONS:

1. In **1-quart saucepan** melt butter over LOW HEAT.
2. Stir in sugar, water, lemon juice, and lemon peel.
3. Stir in beaten eggs and **whisk** quickly to incorporate.
4. Cook over MEDIUM HIGH HEAT, stirring constantly with wire **whisk** until thickened, 5 to 7 minutes.
5. Serve warm over gingerbread, ice cream, or pound cake. YIELD: 2 cups

WHAT WE LEARNED:

✓ An old flavor combination—gingerbread and lemon—brought back to life.

✓ You have to be careful when adding raw egg to a recipe. If you add it directly to something that's hot, the egg might start to scramble. That's why, in this sauce, you whisk the beaten eggs quickly to incorporate into the sauce. You don't want bits of scrambled egg in your dessert. Once it's incorporated, it's fine.

Pop quiz: What is in this recipe that makes the sauce thick?

Answer: the eggs

★

BAILEY'S HOT FUDGE SAUCE – Stovetop

★ MODERATELY EASY

Bailey's Ice Cream was founded in Boston in 1873. Their specialty was the hot fudge sundae, which was served in a silver stemmed cup on a silver plate with a long spoon. The hot fudge was glopped on and dripped lusciously onto the plate. It was chocolate heaven. Unfortunately, its new owner closed the shops in the 1980s, but the recipe lives on. This looks slightly different than what may be the official one, but having sampled their wares before they closed, this is darned close.

INGREDIENTS:

2-1/2 oz. semi-sweet chocolate

½ oz. **unsweetened** chocolate

½ cup (1 stick) butter

2 cups confectioner's sugar

¾ cup (6 oz. or small can) evaporated milk

DIRECTIONS:

1. In **heavy saucepan**, melt butter and chocolate over MEDIUM-HIGH HEAT. DON'T WALK AWAY or it may burn!
2. Remove from heat.
3. Add confectioner's sugar and evaporated milk, stirring with a **whisk** until smooth.
4. Return to heat.
5. Cook 8 to 10 minutes over MEDIUM HEAT, stirring frequently. DON'T WALK AWAY! Sauce may bubble even over low heat.
6. Will thicken further upon standing. Keep refrigerated. When ready to use, heat in microwave at 80% for 30 seconds.

WHAT WE LEARNED:

✓ Patience in staying with this expensive-ingredient sauce until it's done.

✓ Try different strengths and types of chocolate just for fun.

★

SALTED CARAMEL ICE CREAM TOPPING - Stovetop

★ EASY

INGREDIENTS:

1 cup firmly packed brown sugar

¾ cup butter (1-1/2 sticks)

1-1/2 T. water

1 tsp. sea salt

¾ tsp. baking soda

½ tsp. vanilla extract

DIRECTIONS:

1. In **large saucepan** over MEDIUM HEAT, combine sugar, butter, water, and salt.
2. Cook until melted and bubbly around the edge, stirring frequently. Continue cooking 2 more minutes, stirring frequently.
3. Remove from heat; stir in baking soda and vanilla. Stir until caramel darkens in color (about 1-2 minutes).
4. Let stand 1 minute. Topping will harden slightly when poured over ice cream.

WHIPPED CREAM – electric mixer on stand or hand mixer

★ MODERATELY EASY

This isn't particularly time consuming, but you need to follow the directions exactly if you want fluffy, not flat, homemade whipped cream.

This recipe calls for Heavy Cream. You will also see Whipping Cream on the shelves. Both are good for making homemade whipped cream, but the Heavy Cream has slightly more butterfat in it and is more stable because of that.

INGREDIENTS:

1 cup Heavy Cream

1 tsp. vanilla extract

1 T. sugar – or to taste

DIRECTIONS:

1. Chill **mixing bowl and beaters** in freezer for 10 minutes. This is important.
2. Pour cream in chilled bowl and beat with **electric mixer** on MEDIUM-HIGH until soft peaks form. Soft peaks are when the peaks curl down when the beaters are lifted up.
3. Add vanilla extract and sugar.
4. Beat a bit longer on HIGH SPEED just until peaks stiffen—or hold their shape when you lift up the mixer.
5. DO NOT OVERBEAT or it will turn to butter. Make close to serving time.

WHAT WE LEARNED:

✓ The difference between Heavy Cream and Whipping Cream (just a few percentage points of butterfat)

✓ That when making a recipe like this, you should follow the directions exactly. Unlike some of my other recipes, this is no place for experimentation.

★

COOKIES

SWEET DREAM CHOCOLATE CHIP COOKIES – Preheat oven to 375°F

★ **MODERATELY EASY**

INGREDIENTS:

2 sticks butter – *room temperature*

1-1/2 cups brown sugar, tightly packed into measuring cup

1 egg – *room temperature*

2 cups flour

1 tsp. baking soda

1 tsp. cinnamon

1 tsp. ground ginger

12 oz. pkg. chocolate chips

1 cup walnuts – *chopped*

1 cup confectioner's sugar (aka powdered) – for rolling

DIRECTIONS:

1. In **large mixing bowl**, mix all ingredients except confectioner's sugar. Refrigerate till firm.
2. Form into 1-inch balls. Use a **small ice cream scoop** for uniformity.
3. Put confectioner's sugar into **small bowl**. Dredge balls through sugar.
4. Put on GREASED **baking sheets,** 2 inches apart, and bake 10 minutes.
5. Cool 5 minutes on baking sheet, then remove and put directly on **wire rack**.
6. If freezing for future use, freeze uncooked, then bake as directed.

WHAT WE LEARNED:

✓ Making cookies requires a strong arm to mix the batter. It helps if the butter is room temperature (not melted).

✓ Never overbake cookies. When they are cooled on baking sheet for a few minutes, they continue to bake a little. They also firm up when cooled.

✓ This recipe has a lot of butter, yet we ask you to grease the baking sheet. These cookies are dredged in sugar and might stick to the pan if you don't.

✓ Most baking sheets hold only about 12 cookies. They spread when cooking. That's why you give them plenty of room.

★

OATMEAL CHOCOLATE CHIP COOKIES – Preheat oven to 375°F

★ **MODERATELY EASY**

INGREDIENTS:

2 sticks butter – *softened*

1-1/4 cups firmly packed brown sugar

½ cup granulated white sugar

2 eggs - *beaten*

2 T. milk

2 tsp. vanilla extract

1-3/4 cups flour

1 tsp. baking soda

½ tsp. salt

2-1/2 cups oatmeal, quick OR old fashioned – *uncooked*

2 cups semi-sweet chocolate morsels

Optional: 1 cup walnuts – *coarsely chopped*

DIRECTIONS:

1. Mix ingredients for cookies using a **whisk, then a big spoon (not a mixer)**.
2. In a **large mixing bowl**, beat butter and both sugars till creamy.
3. Add eggs, milk, and vanilla; beat well.
4. Add flour, baking soda, and salt; mix well.
5. Stir in oats, chocolate chips and nuts; mix well.
6. Drop by rounded measuring tablespoonfuls onto UNGREASED **cookie sheet**.
7. Bake 7 to 9 minutes (convection oven) OR 9 to 10 minutes in regular oven for a chewy cookie. Bake 12 to 13 minutes for a crispy cookie.
8. Cool cookies for 1 minute on cookie sheet, then move to **wire rack**.

WHAT WE LEARNED:

✓ When making cookies, combine wet ingredients and dry ingredients in stages for even mixing, then add the chunky stuff—like nuts, chocolate chips, etc.

✓ Most baking sheets hold only about 12 cookies. They spread when cooking. That's why you give them plenty of room.

OSV MOLASSES COCONUT CHEWS – Preheat oven to 375°F

★ MODERATELY EASY

This is an Olde Sturbridge Village recipe. Your kitchen will smell like an 1840's farmhouse. Like the cartoon character sniffing the cooling pie on the windowsill, people will be drawn to your kitchen when you bake these.

INGREDIENTS:

1 cup white granulated sugar

1 cup brown sugar, firmly packed

1 cup shortening (like canned Crisco)

2 eggs – *beaten*

2 tsp. vanilla extract

¼ cup molasses

4 cups sifted flour

1 tsp. salt

1-1/2 tsp. baking soda

1 cup coconut flakes

DIRECTIONS:

1. In **large mixing bowl**, cream together the white sugar, brown sugar, and shortening, using a **whisk or large spoon**.
2. Add beaten eggs, vanilla, and molasses. Beat well.
3. In a **separate medium-sized mixing bowl**, use a **flour sifter** to sift together the flour, baking soda, and salt. Stir into sugar mixture.
4. Stir in coconut flakes.
5. Shape into small balls and place 3 inches apart on a GREASED **cookie sheet**.
6. Bake at 375°F for 12-15 minutes. Do not overbake.
7. Cool on cookie sheet for 1 minute, then transfer cookies directly to **wire rack**.
8. YIELD: about 3 dozen.

WHAT WE LEARNED:

✓ What shortening is. This is used in place of butter.

✓ What a flour sifter is. It evens out the dry ingredients and sifts out any lumps. If you don't have one, it will still turn out okay; just dump in the dry ingredients.

★

MAGNIFICENT MOCHA BROWNIES – Preheat oven to 325°F

★ MODERATELY EASY

INGREDIENTS:

1/3 cup butter (5-1/3 Tablespoons)

¾ cup white granulated sugar

2 T. water

12 oz. bag chocolate chips – *divided*

1 tsp. vanilla

¾ cup flour

2 tsp. espresso powder (found in baking aisle)

¼ tsp. baking soda

Pinch of salt

2 eggs – *beaten*

½ cup walnuts – *chopped*

DIRECTIONS:

1. In a **small saucepan**, combine butter, sugar, and water. Bring to a boil.
2. Add 1 cup of chocolate chips and vanilla. Immediately remove from heat and beat with **whisk** till chocolate is melted and smooth.
3. Pour chocolate mixture into a **large mixing bowl**.
4. Add flour, espresso powder, baking soda, and salt; mix well.
5. Add eggs, one at a time; beat well.
6. Add remaining chocolate chips and nuts.
7. GREASE bottom only of an **8" or 9" square brownie pan**. Pour batter into pan and bake 25-30 minutes. Do not overbake as they will firm up when cool.

WHAT WE LEARNED:

✓ Be careful when adding raw egg to a recipe. If you add it directly to something that's hot, the egg might start to scramble. Add the flour, etc. first to cool things down, THEN add the eggs to avoid scrambled egg in your dessert.

✓ Greasing pan <u>bottom only</u> helps it rise, and it just naturally pulls away from the sides slightly when done.[11]

KID AGAIN BROWNIES – Preheat oven to 350°F

★ **MODERATELY EASY** – This is a peanut butter & jelly square the kids will love!

INGREDIENTS:

½ cup organic peanut butter

1/3 cup butter (5-1/3 Tablespoons) – *room temperature*

1 cup white granulated sugar

¼ cup brown sugar

2 eggs – *beaten*

1 cup flour

1 tsp. baking powder

¼ tsp. salt

½ tsp. vanilla extract

2 tsp. light or white corn syrup (looks clear)

1 cup peanut butter chips

DIRECTIONS:

1. In a **large mixing bowl**, mix peanut butter and butter with **whisk**.
2. Gradually add sugars; mix well.
3. Add eggs, one at a time; mix well.
4. Using a **sifter**, sift dry ingredients into bowl; mix well, using a spoon.
5. Add vanilla and 2 tsp. of corn syrup; mix well. Lastly, add peanut butter chips.
6. Pour into **9" square pan**, GREASED ON BOTTOM ONLY. Bake 30 minutes (convection oven) or till tester/toothpick comes out clean. Cool on rack completely before frosting with peanut butter frosting (see *Dessert Sauces and Frostings* chapter.) After frosting, squiggle jelly over the top.

WHAT WE LEARNED:

✓ Use organic peanut butter, which is just peanuts and salt. Others may contain sugars or trans-fats, which you don't need.

✓ If you don't want to grease the pan, use parchment paper, draped up the sides. Then when it cools, you pick it up like handles and plop onto your rack or cutting board quite easily.

★

MOM'S GRAHAM CRACKER SQUARES – Preheat oven to 350°F

★ RIDICULOUSLY EASY

INGREDIENTS:

18 graham crackers OR = to 1-1/2 cups crushed

1 can condensed milk (no substitutions!)

½ cup sweetened coconut

1 cup chocolate bits

DIRECTIONS:

1. In a **large mixing bowl**, mix all ingredients with a big spoon.
2. Spread in GREASED 9" x 13" pan.
3. Bake at 350°F for 25 minutes.

WHAT WE LEARNED:

✓ Condensed milk is evaporated milk with sugar added.[12] It is a very specific product which goes by either Sweetened Condensed Milk or just Condensed Milk. It comes in cans.

★

PARTY TIPS

I SAVED THIS CHAPTER for last, kind of a graduation day, for my aspiring chef students. Now that you've cooked and learned how to prepare delicious food, it's time to show off. Let's be honest. As someone who likes to cook, you need an audience. All that learning, cooking, and washing up should be rewarded.

And luckily for all of us, your friends and families are waiting in the wings dying to be invited over to help you out with that. There are so many ways to go. You can knock yourself out preparing labor-intensive recipes if you like. You can just buy takeout and set it out in your prettiest dishes. Or you can do a combination of both. It doesn't matter. What matters is that you cruise into the adult world with a generosity of spirit and take care of people by organizing and providing a meal.

The younger generation keeps saying "adulting is hard." But learning and becoming better at something is challenging and fun. The sense of empowerment you get is worth it. Frankly, it's just <u>not</u> all that hard and it should stop being said. People do one thing at a time like every other generation and they get there. No one is born knowing things. People in the 1840s went out West in a covered wagon with their few worldly goods, looked for sources of water, camped out every night, withstood Indian raids and snakes, and it took 6 months of that to get to California. Half the time, they had a baby on the way. Then when they finally got there, they had to fell some trees and build a cabin. <u>Now</u> do you think adulting is hard?

But back to parties. One thing that continues to baffle me is why the scenes I see in movies are supposed to constitute a "party" when all I see is a bunch of snarky people grimly holding onto a red plastic cup full of booze. There is never a bite of food in sight, which is probably why the attendees end up in an argument, pushing someone into the swimming pool, or other mayhem. You can call it a party if you want but I don't want. I'm Italian and I'm sorry but if you don't provide food it's not a party.

- It should be stated here that guests may have allergies or are vegetarian or some variation thereof. Try to determine ahead of time so you provide at least something they will like to eat. Use vegetable broth instead of meat broth, etc. Serve salads and make some dishes without meat.

- If a casual get-together, buy some heavy-duty paper plates and cups in a seasonal theme. Set out plastic utensils, napkins and toothpicks.

Here are some entertaining ideas:

EASY

Summer: Order a party platter along with bread or rolls from a grocery store several days in advance of your party. Or make your own sandwiches, cut the crusts off, and cut into small triangles. People love these. Buy some soda, iced tea, potato salad, cole slaw, potato chips, and ice cream. Buy beer or wine if consumed.

Make-your-own-sundae dessert:

1. Make the Bailey's Hot Fudge sauce and the Salted Caramel Sauce recipes.
2. Cut up some fresh strawberries and put in a bowl with white granulated sugar poured over it (2 T to ¼ cup depending on preference). It will be strawberry sauce in about an hour.
3. Set out bowls, spoons, ice cream scoop, the 3 sauces, the ice cream, a bowl of chopped walnuts, and a can of whipped cream.

Winter: Order a party platter. Order some chowder, soup, or chili from the grocery store or your favorite restaurant. Put the soup into a crockpot(s). Buy pre-made frozen meatballs and put in another crockpot; pour a jar or two of tomato sauce over it. Make a few quiches. These are satisfying and easy to serve in wedges. Or maybe a casserole, which serves many.

Serve a pre-made cake for dessert, or mini-cupcakes. One good way to serve cake, as one caterer told me, was to make a large cake, then cut into squares small enough to fit into a cupcake liner. Guests can just grab it, and even eat out of the liner if they can't find a fork.

Or you could order Chinese takeout, or a lasagna from your favorite place and serve with a tossed salad.

OPEN HOUSE:

I love a winter holiday-themed open house. You can decorate the house, guests come and go, there is a nice buzz of people talking, and you get to show off your cooking skills. Since you will host a large-ish amount of people, they won't necessarily be sitting down unless they can find one of the few spots in your home. That is why you will make sure you have sturdy or real plates, finger foods, or food that's easy to eat (obviously not steak filets).

So many things can go in the crockpot, which also keeps things hot when it's meal time. If you have something in a casserole dish, a warming hotplate is very handy. The following suggestions are all things you can make ahead and dump into the crockpot, or make cookie sheet panfuls in large quantities and just set out.

ITALIAN THEMED:

1. Crockpot—Applesauce meatballs with the tomato sauce.
2. Pasta, preferably something like penne or bowties (Farfalle) because they're easier to eat than vermicelli when you're standing up.
3. Caesar salad (chopped), maybe with your own Caesar salad dressing.
4. Buy a nice loaf of Italian bread, set out with pats of butter.
5. Dessert—I can see this combo with the Éclair Ring recipe, the German Sweet Chocolate Pie or the Magnificent Mocha Brownies. Yum. What time do you want me?

Cajun themed:

1. Crockpot—Jambalaya
2. Crabbies
3. Sausage Cheeseballs
4. Greta's Corn Bread
5. Dessert—Banana Bread Pudding or Chocolate Banana Pudding Pie

Greek themed:

1. Crockpot—Spiced Lamb Meatballs
2. Rice pilaf
3. Greek salad (chopped) with Yasou® dressing or your own Greek salad dressing
4. Dessert—a Lemon Pudding Cake or buy some baklava.

General Ideas:

> Baked beans in a crockpot is welcomed with just about any food.

> Trifle is just cake and a few other things in a tall glass dish. It always looks fancy.

> Tiny sandwiches with the crusts cut off are always big hits. They're easy to eat standing up.

There are endless themes you can put together, which is really fun.

DINNER PARTY:

This is more formal. You invite specific people and plan your meal accordingly. This is <u>not</u> a see-who-drops-in kind of meal.

1. Don't try a new recipe on company. Use your tried-and-true recipes.
2. Whatever food you plan, picture how it will look on the plate. Aim for different textures and colors. For example, you wouldn't want scallops in a white sauce, mashed potatoes, and cauliflower, with vanilla ice cream for dessert. Too much white! Aim for a more colorful plate. If you serve creamy things, pick something crispy to go with it.
3. Set the table ahead of time. Use cloth napkins if you have them. The place setting utensils is set up that food eaten first goes on the outside then you work your way inside. So salad fork on the outside left, then dinner fork on the immediate left of the plate. Dinner knife and spoon on the right of the plate.

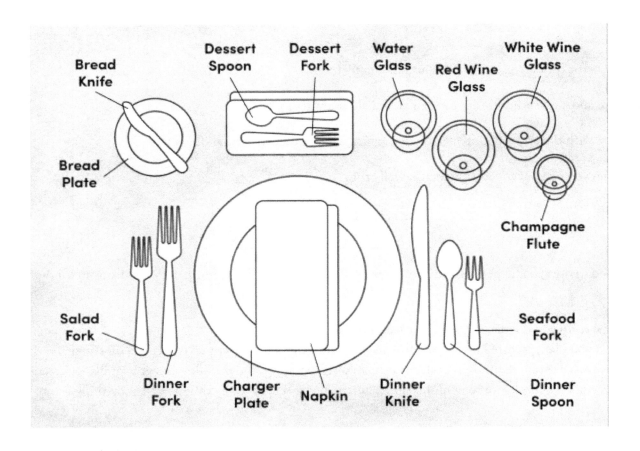

1. State a specific time for guests to arrive, like 6:00 pm.

2. Arrange your appetizers/cocktails for 6:00, with dinner for 6:30 or 7:00 pm.

3. Have someone help guests with parking if that's an issue. That will make your guests feel welcomed and in a better mood if they know their cars won't be towed!

4. Greet your guests at the door. Hang up their coats. Get them a drink.

5. Introduce them to each other if necessary. Let them enjoy the appetizers and drinks while you finish up the dinner in the kitchen. If you've invited a livewire type person, let them entertain everyone while you're busy. This is a good thing.

6. If you're having just a few people over, you may want to serve the food family style, which means big serving dishes that get passed around. If you're have a bigger crowd—say 6 to 8, you may want to put all the food out buffet style on a counter or table. They pick up a dish, form a line, and help themselves, then go sit at the table. Some people prefer this.

7. For dessert, I set up a dessert station in another room. I then have the room to cut the cake, dish out ice cream, etc.

8. Offer the guests coffee, either regular or decaf, and tea. Offer milk, cream, sweetener and put on the table so they can make it their way.

9. If you have a lot of leftovers, it's nice to prepare a doggie bag for each guest. If you don't have many leftovers or don't want to part with it, just don't, as guests don't usually expect it.

10. If something goes wrong, don't apologize for it, as it just draws more attention to your problem. When I was a newlywed, I once invited 6 people over and I presented a roast chicken with the usual side dishes. What I failed to realize was that a small roast chicken serves about 3 people. I started to panic as I saw the guests politely taking tiny amounts of chicken. I went back to the kitchen and brought out more of something to fill them up, but I didn't make an issue out of it because I was so embarrassed. I did have a big dessert, so hopefully that helped.

KITCHEN PROTOCOLS:

1. When you are the cook in your own kitchen, you are in charge. You make the decisions. Other people usually know this and defer to you as the Captain of the kitchen. They will do what you tell them—whether it be your request to help out or get out of your way. You, of course, will offer them the same courtesy when you go over to their house when they reciprocate, which they will as polite members of society.

2. If someone asks you to bring something, you are all set, having read this cookbook. There must be something you like to make. Ask your hostess what she'd like and try to oblige. Someone else may be bringing the dessert, so if she asks you to bring an appetizer, do so. Don't compete with the other dessert-bringer.

3. If someone leaves a cake tote at your house, wash it well and give back to them as soon as possible. Don't be like my neighbor, who hung on to my $50 special cake tote until I had to go to her house and finally get it back a month later.

And, lastly, having given you instructions on how to host a party, if you just can't deal with all the preparation, cooking, and cleaning up, do this. Just offer to take your friends—to whom you may owe a dinner—out to eat, your treat, *which you will specify clearly up front*. That is certainly easy and fun, and takes care of your reciprocating obligation. People notice those things. Yeah, they do. Don't be like some people we know who "invited" us out to the husband's birthday dinner an hour away. Here comes the check and all the other guests start fishing for their wallets. Why did I sense that coming? Luckily it was a rare occasion when I had a few hundred dollars in cash on me. Not cool. If you invite someone out as your guest, YOU pay. If you can't afford it, either don't go out or make it plain up front.

Certainly there is much much more information on cooking techniques out there. This book is intended to get you started. Learning is a lifelong journey. Patience, young grasshopper.

THE END

[1] SERVSAFE.COM, AN EDUCATIONAL program sponsored by the National Restaurant Association.

[2] Report by the Institute of Food Technologists for the Food and Drug Administration of the United States Department of Health and Human Services

[3] https://www.lawinsider.com/dictionary/potentially-hazardous-foods

[4] https://www.thespruceeats.com/easy-fried-fish-fillets-3056505

[5] https://spoonuniversity.com/lifestyle/does-alcohol-cook-out

[6] Better Homes & Gardens online article, *When to Use Glass or Metal Pans for Every Type of Recipe,*

July 24, 2020

[7] *New York Times* recipe adapted from Greg Collier, chef and co-owner of Leah & Louise, Charlotte, NC.

[8] https://gramsrecipebox.com/2011/04/04/watergate-cake/

[9] www.finecooking.com/article/why-bake-custards-in[1] a water bath

[10] www.finecooking.com/article/why-bake-custards-in[2] a water bath

---

1. http://www.finecooking.com/article/why-bake-custards-in

2. http://www.finecooking.com/article/why-bake-custards-in

[11] https://www.lodinews.com/lodi_living/food_and_wine/columnists/barbara_spitzer/article_b095ad4e-6992-11e3-b587-0019bb2963f4.html

[12] https://www.merriam-webster.com/dictionary/condensed%20milk

Don't miss out!

Visit the website below and you can sign up to receive emails whenever Lavinia M. Hughes publishes a new book. There's no charge and no obligation.

https://books2read.com/r/B-A-GFFO-CQLTB

About the Author

Lavinia M. Hughes, a native New Englander, has been a foodie since junior high school taking every cooking class she could find. Her love of food and cooking started with a cashier and food prep job at a fast-food restaurant, transitioned to a grocery cashier, and continued to complete cooking courses in Lebanese, Chinese, Caribbean, and Italian cooking, cake decorating, and even more hands-on courses at The Kitchen in Waitsfield, VT, taught by Johnson & Wales-trained chefs.

She worked as a secretary to the Director of Product Development at a major food franchisor, setting up taste tests and analyzing sales figures from test marketing of new products, obtaining food samples required in testing a new offering; and meeting with salespeople introducing new food items.

She completed a Serv-Safe (Mass. Dept. of Agriculture) course, toured local restaurants with the health inspector, and completed a 3-day hands-on Food Safety Seminar at a local hotel.

As Office Manager in her family-owned safety consulting and training business, she managed catering to large classes of students.

An ardent student of The Great Courses, she continues to take cooking courses taught by CIA-trained Chef Bill Briwa or the history of food taught by Professor Ken Albala, Ph.D.

She is the author of **Enter Through the Crawlspace**, a compilation of 20 short stories in the paranormal genre, available on all digital platforms. With her husband, she has co-authored a novel **Newtucket – the Rising**, available on all digital platforms, as well as seven screenplays: *Cape Car Blues, Freeport Fred's Valiant Summer, Golf Cart Ranger, Plimsoll, Training Ship, What We Can't Know,* and *Get Togethe*r, loglines of which are available at http://RichardGHughes.superscreenplay.com

She lives and writes with her husband, fellow author Richard Hughes, in the seaside village of Waquoit on Cape Cod.

About the Publisher

Waquoit Wordsmith Press, located in a small seaside village on Cape Cod.
Cover art by: Rebekah Sather, SelfPubBookCovers.com. RebekahSather@1stFruitsDesign

CPSIA information can be obtained
at www.ICGtesting.com
Printed in the USA
JSHW041131110622
26814JS00005B/73

9 798201 691301